Export & Import Documentation Simplified

A Handbook of Samples, Templates, & Tips!

Yoshi Mori

ATTACHÉ BOOKS

ATTACHÉ BOOKS

Manufactured in the United States of America

10 9 8 7 6 5 4 3 2 1

Library of Congress Cataloging-in-Publication Data

Mori, Yoshi.
Export & Import Documentation Simplified: A Handbook of Samples, Templates, & Tips! / Yoshi Mori.

Business & Economics, Exports & Imports

ISBN-13: 978-0615783635
ISBN-10: 0615783635

The internet web addresses referenced in this book were confirmed to be valid and correct at the time of the book's publication but may be subject to change.

Contents (at a Glance)

Disclaimer:

This book is designed to provide expert guidance regarding the subject matter covered. This information is given with the understanding that neither the author nor the publisher is engaged in rendering legal, accounting, or other professional advice. Since the details of your situation are fact dependent, you should also seek the advice of a competent professional.

All samples and templates contained herein are at the complete disposal of the owner of this book. Some of the templates contained in this book may be replicated by making multiple facsimile copies of a form or forms for repetitive use, or by carefully detaching the 8.8" x 11" pages from their binding. Though the utmost care was put into the creation of each sample and template, some templates will not be directly suitable for use as official documents. For example, both the Bill of Lading and Cargo Insurance Certificate must be issued by the cargo carrier and insurance company respectively.

1
Intro (in Brief)

What this book IS...

- A cheat sheet-like, easy-to-read overview of each of the most popular types of import & export documents in use today
- Thorough yet concise dissection of a wide variety of the most prevalently used shipping docs and forms
- Formatted for a side-by-side comparison of all blank forms vs. all correctly completed forms
- A compilation of documents completed in a manner most commonly practiced
- A practitioner's (not theorist's) guide to real-world import & export documentation
- Easy to navigate from one form to the next
- Complete with a robust index for quick reference and lookups
- International business simplified

What this book IS NOT...

- A collection of exhaustive ramblings on how a dictionary defines each document
- Inclusive of irrelevant documents and parts thereof so commonly used on documents
- Laced with outdated theory and terminology
- Solely for the experienced veteran of international documentation

2

Air Waybill (AWB)

Arrival Notice (A/N)
Bill of Lading (BL)
Booking Request
Cargo Insurance Certificate (COI)
Certificate of Origin (COO)
Commercial Invoice (CI)
Declaration for Free Entry of Returned U.S. Goods (USGR)
Declaration of No Wood Packing Material (WPM)
Declaration of Non-Coniferous Wood Packing Material (WPM)
Entry Summary (Customs Form 7501)
Importer Security Filing Form (ISF)
Importer's Blanket Statement of Non-Reimbursement of Anti-Dumping Duties (AD/CVD)
Letter of Credit Application (L/C)
Packing List (PL)
Power of Attorney (POA)
Pre-Shipment Inspection Certificate (PSIC)
Pro Forma Invoice
Purchase Order (PO)
Sales Order (SO)
Shipping Instructions (SI)
Telex Release Request (TLX)
Toxic Substances Control Act Statement (TSCA)

Air Waybill (AWB)

ALSO KNOWN AS:
AWB. Air Consignment Note.

REQUIRED FOR:
All Air Imports and Exports

NOT REQUIRED FOR:
N/A

ORIGINAL COPIES NORMALLY REQUIRED?:
No

IN SUMMARY:
The air waybill is issued by the shipping company to the shipper, and serves the following purposes...

- It confirms the shipping company's receipt of goods tendered to it by the shipper.
- It exists as a contract between the shipper and the shipping company outlining the agreement to deliver the freight as per the air waybill.
- It communicates information regarding the consignee and notify parties at destination, airline routing and flight details, and handling instructions as per the shipper's instructions.

USEFUL TIPS:
The International Air Transport Association (IATA) is the air cargo industry's trade group. It is comprised of international and domestic airline companies and it maintains the specifications and uniformity of international air transport tools such as the air waybill. More on the air waybill can be found on IATA's website.

https://www.iata.org/whatwedo/cargo/pages/air_waybill.aspx

WHAT TO REMEMBER:
Unlike the ocean bill of lading, the air waybill is always non-negotiable, meaning that the original copy does not constitute title of the shipped goods.

Shipper's Name and Address	Shipper's Account Number ( )	Air Waybill
		Copies 1, 2 and 3 of this Air Waybill are originals and have the same validity
Consignee's Name and Address	Consignee's Account Number ( )	It is agreed that the goods described herein are accepted in apparent good order and condition (except as noted) for carriage SUBJECT TO THE CONDITIONS OF CONTRACT ON THE REVERSE HEREOF. ALL GOODS MAY BE CARRIED BY ANY OTHER MEANS INCLUDING ROAD OR ANY OTHER CARRIER UNLESS SPECIFIC CONTRARY INSTRUCTIONS ARE GIVEN HEREON BY THE SHIPPER, AND SHIPPER AGREES THAT THE SHIPMENT MAY BE CARRIED VIA INTERMEDIATE STOPPING PLACES WHICH THE CARRIER DEEMS APPROPRIATE. THE SHIPPER'S ATTENTION IS DRAWN TO THE NOTICE CONCERNING CARRIER'S LIMITATION OF LIABILITY. Shipper may increase such limitation of liability by declaring a higher value for carriage and paying a supplemental charge if required.
Issuing carrier's agent name and city		Accounting Information
Agent's IATA Code	Account No.	
Airport of Departure and Requested Routing		Reference Number

To	By First Carrier (Routing and Destination)	Currency	CHGS Code	PPD	COLL	Declared Value for Carriage	Declared Value for Customs

Airport of Destination	Requested Flight/Date	Amount of Insurance	INSURANCE – If carrier offers Insurance, and such Insurance is requested in accordance with the conditions thereof, Indicate amount to be insured in figures in box marked "Amount of Insurance".

Handling Information

No. of Pieces RCP	Gross Weight	kg lb	Rate Class	Commodity Item no.	Chargeable Weight	Rate/ Charge	Total	Nature and quantity of goods (Incl. dimensions or volume)

(Prepaid) (Weight Charge) (Collect)	Other Charges
(Valuation Charge)	
(Tax)	I hereby certify that the particulars on the face hereof are correct and that insofar as any part of the consignment contains dangerous goods, such part is properly described by name and is in proper condition for carriage by air according to the applicable Dangerous Goods Regulations.
(Total Other Charges Due Agent)	
(Total Other Charges Due Carrier)	Signature of Shipper or his Agent
(Total Prepaid) (Total Collect)	
(Currency Conversion) (CC Charges in Dest. Currency)	Executed on (Date) (Place) Signature of Issuing Carrier or Its Agent

For Carrier's Use only at Destination	(Charges at Destination)	(Total Collect Charges)

(Sample)

000-0000 0000 | 000-0000 0000

Shipper's Name and Address
ABC CO., INC.
1234 A ST.
ANYTOWN, USA

Shipper's Account Number
( )

Air Waybill

Issued by Joe's Shipping Co. JSC

Copies 1, 2 and 3 of this Air Waybill are originals and have the same validity

It is agreed that the goods described herein are accepted in apparent good order and condition (except as noted) for carriage SUBJECT TO THE CONDITIONS OF CONTRACT ON THE REVERSE HEREOF. ALL GOODS MAY BE CARRIED BY ANY OTHER MEANS INCLUDING ROAD OR ANY OTHER CARRIER UNLESS SPECIFIC CONTRARY INSTRUCTIONS ARE GIVEN HEREON BY THE SHIPPER, AND SHIPPER AGREES THAT THE SHIPMENT MAY BE CARRIED VIA INTERMEDIATE STOPPING PLACES WHICH THE CARRIER DEEMS APPROPRIATE. THE SHIPPER'S ATTENTION IS DRAWN TO THE NOTICE CONCERNING CARRIER'S LIMITATION OF LIABILITY. Shipper may increase such limitation of liability by declaring a higher value for carriage and paying a supplemental charge if required.

Consignee's Name and Address
BEST SPORTS CO., LTD.
888 OMOTE-DORI,
YOKOHAMA, JAPAN
TEL: (XXX) XXX - XXXX
FAX: (XXX) XXX - XXXX

Consignee's Account Number
( )

Issuing carrier's agent name and city

Accounting Information

Agent's IATA Code	Account No.

Airport of Departure and Requested Routing
LOS ANGELES (LAX)

Reference Number
PO 1234

To	By First Carrier (Routing and Destination)
NRT	JS

Currency	CHGS Code	PPD	COLL	Declared Value for Carriage	Declared Value for Customs
USD		X		NVD	$10,000.00 USD

Airport of Destination	Requested Flight/Date	Amount of Insurance
NARITA (NRT)	JS123/01	NIL

INSURANCE – If carrier offers Insurance, and such Insurance is requested in accordance with the conditions thereof, Indicate amount to be insured in figures in box marked "Amount of Insurance".

Handling Information
Please Notify Consignee to Pick up. These commodities, technology, or software were exported from the United States in accordance with the Export Administration Regulations. Diversion contrary to U.S. law prohibited.

No. of Pieces RCP	Gross Weight	kg lb	Rate Class	Commodity Item no.	Chargeable Weight	Rate/ Charge	Total	Nature and quantity of goods (Incl. dimensions or volume)
1000	204	K	K		309			SPORTS EQUIPMENT (BASKETBALLS & VOLLEYBALLS) DIMS: 1 @ 102X102X102 CM 1 @ 102X102X76 CM

(Prepaid)	(Weight Charge)	(Collect)
PREPAID		
	(Valuation Charge)	
	(Tax)	
	(Total Other Charges Due Agent)	
	(Total Other Charges Due Carrier)	
(Total Prepaid) $900.00 USD		(Total Collect)
(Currency Conversion)		(CC Charges in Dest. Currency)

Other Charges

I hereby certify that the particulars on the face hereof are correct and that insofar as any part of the consignment contains dangerous goods, such part is properly described by name and is in proper condition for carriage by air according to the applicable Dangerous Goods Regulations.

Signature of Shipper or his Agent

Executed on (Date) (Place) Signature of Issuing Carrier or Its Agent

For Carrier's Use only at Destination	(Charges at Destination)	(Total Collect Charges)

000-0000 0000

3

Air Waybill (AWB)

Arrival Notice (A/N)

Bill of Lading (BL)
Booking Request
Cargo Insurance Certificate (COI)
Certificate of Origin (COO)
Commercial Invoice (CI)
Declaration for Free Entry of Returned U.S. Goods (USGR)
Declaration of No Wood Packing Material (WPM)
Declaration of Non-Coniferous Wood Packing Material (WPM)
Entry Summary (Customs Form 7501)
Importer Security Filing Form (ISF)
Importer's Blanket Statement of Non-Reimbursement of Anti-Dumping Duties (AD/CVD)
Letter of Credit Application (L/C)
Packing List (PL)
Power of Attorney (POA)
Pre-Shipment Inspection Certificate (PSIC)
Pro Forma Invoice
Purchase Order (PO)
Sales Order (SO)
Shipping Instructions (SI)
Telex Release Request (TLX)
Toxic Substances Control Act Statement (TSCA)

Arrival Notice (A/N)

ALSO KNOWN AS:
A/N. Notice of Arrival.

REQUIRED FOR:
All Imports

NOT REQUIRED FOR:
N/A

ORIGINAL COPIES NORMALLY REQUIRED?:
No.

IN SUMMARY:
Carriers will routinely and automatically send written notification of a shipment's upcoming importation in the form of an arrival notice. The arrival notice is emailed, faxed, and/or snail mailed to the "shipper" and "notify party" entities as listed on the bill of lading or air waybill.

USEFUL TIPS:
Ask your customer (the exporter/shipper) to email a copy of the bill of lading to you as soon as it is available from the carrier at origin. The bill of lading is normally available within a day or two from the date of departure from the foreign port of lading. With information from the bill of lading on hand, the importer can follow-up with the carrier to ensure that a timely arrival notice will be sent to the appropriate parties at destination.

WHAT TO REMEMBER:
The importer should take special note of the arrival notice's 1) cargo pickup location and 2) estimated arrival date at destination in order to prevent costly, yet avoidable, storage charges (also known as "demurrage") at the port of import. Demurrage begins to accrue on a daily basis immediately after the "last free day". The last free day at destination may or may not be included on the carrier's arrival notice, and can be confirmed by contacting the carrier as per their contact instructions as notated on the arrival notice.

ARRIVAL NOTICE

JSC JOE'S SHIPPING CO.

SHIPPER	BL NO. BOOKING NO.
	EXPORT REFERENCES
CONSIGNEE	MAIL NOTICE OF ARRIVAL TO
NOTIFY	CARGO PICKUP LOCATION

ETA AT PORT OF DISCHARGE	COMBINED TRANSPORT - PLACE OF RECEIPT
VESSEL AND VOYAGE	PORT OF LOADING
PORT OF DISCHARGE	COMBINED TRANSPORT - PLACE OF DELIVERY

MARKS AND NUMBERS	NO. OF PKGS.	DESCRIPTION OF GOODS	GRS WEIGHT	MEASUREMENT

FREIGHT & CHARGES	RATE	PER	AMOUNT	PREPAID	COLLECT	***CONTACT OFFICE***

(Sample)

ARRIVAL NOTICE

JSC JOE'S SHIPPING CO.

SHIPPER BEST SPORTS, LTD. 888 OMOTE-DORI, YOKOHAMA, JAPAN	**BL NO.** JSCU23456789 **BOOKING NO.** JSCU23456789 **EXPORT REFERENCES** PO#5678
CONSIGNEE ABC CO., INC. 1234 A ST. ANYTOWN, USA	**MAIL NOTICE OF ARRIVAL TO** ABC CO., INC. 1234 A ST. ANYTOWN, USA ATTN: LOGISTICS DEPT.
NOTIFY SAME AS CONSIGNEE TEL: (XXX) XXX - XXXX FAX: (XXX) XXX - XXXX EMAIL: DEE@ABCSPORTY.COM	**CARGO PICKUP LOCATION** PIER XYZ 999 PORT BLVD., LOS ANGELES, CA TEL: (XXX) XXX - XXXX FAX: (XXX) XXX - XXXX
ETA AT PORT OF DISCHARGE 01/01/20XX 12:00 PM	**COMBINED TRANSPORT - PLACE OF RECEIPT**
VESSEL AND VOYAGE JOE EXPRESS V. 002E	**PORT OF LOADING** YOKOHAMA
PORT OF DISCHARGE LOS ANGELES	**COMBINED TRANSPORT - PLACE OF DELIVERY**

MARKS AND NUMBERS	NO. OF PKGS.	DESCRIPTION OF GOODS	GRS WEIGHT	MEASUREMENT
"BEST SPORTS JAPAN" CONTAINER NO. JSCU1234567 SEAL NO. 2468	1000 BOXES ON 2 PALLETS	SPORTS EQUIPMENT (BASEBALLS)	150.000 KGS	2 CBM

FREIGHT & CHARGES	RATE	PER	AMOUNT	PREPAID	COLLECT
OCEAN FREIGHT			AS ARRANGED	X	
ADDL. FEES ORIGIN			AS ARRANGED	X	
THC DESTINATION	50.00 USD	1	50.00 USD		X

CONTACT OFFICE
JOE'S SHIPPING CO.
888 OCEANSIDE ROAD
LOS ANGELES, CA
TEL: (XXX) XXX - XXXX
FAX: (XXX) XXX - XXXX

4

Air Waybill (AWB)
Arrival Notice (A/N)

Bill of Lading (BL)

Booking Request
Cargo Insurance Certificate (COI)
Certificate of Origin (COO)
Commercial Invoice (CI)
Declaration for Free Entry of Returned U.S. Goods (USGR)
Declaration of No Wood Packing Material (WPM)
Declaration of Non-Coniferous Wood Packing Material (WPM)
Entry Summary (Customs Form 7501)
Importer Security Filing Form (ISF)
Importer's Blanket Statement of Non-Reimbursement of Anti-Dumping Duties (AD/CVD)
Letter of Credit Application (L/C)
Packing List (PL)
Power of Attorney (POA)
Pre-Shipment Inspection Certificate (PSIC)
Pro Forma Invoice
Purchase Order (PO)
Sales Order (SO)
Shipping Instructions (SI)
Telex Release Request (TLX)
Toxic Substances Control Act Statement (TSCA)

Bill of Lading (BL)

ALSO KNOWN AS:
Clean Bill of Lading. Non-negotiable or Negotiable Bill of Lading. BOL. BL.

REQUIRED FOR:
All Ocean Imports and Exports

NOT REQUIRED FOR:
N/A

ORIGINAL COPIES NORMALLY REQUIRED?:
The necessity of issuing Original Bills of Lading (OBL) depends on the method of transfer of ownership as agreed upon between shipper and consignee.

IN SUMMARY:
The bill of lading is issued by the shipping company to the shipper, and serves the following purposes…

- It confirms the shipping company's receipt of goods tendered to it by the shipper (usually once loaded on the vessel).
- It exists as a contract between the shipper and the shipping company outlining the agreement to deliver the freight as per the bill of lading.
- It reveals that the importer of record at destination is the consignee party unless otherwise specified.
- It can function as legal title to the merchandise.

USEFUL TIPS:
Confirm beforehand with your customer, the consignee as listed on the bill of lading, regarding what additional details they would like to have included on the BOL.

WHAT TO REMEMBER:
As with all contracts, it is important to explicitly and clearly communicate all of your instructions to the shipping company so that they may properly draft the bill of lading for you accordingly. See the section of this handbook titled "Shipping Instructions (SI)" on how to do so. Request a proof copy of the BOL within a day or two after the sailing of the vessel so that any discrepancies may be corrected prior to the closing of the carrier's manifest.

(VOID—Actual Bill of Lading Must Be From Issuing Carrier) **BILL OF LADING**

SHIPPER	BOOKING NO.
	EXPORT REFERENCES
CONSIGNEE	FORWARDING AGENT REFERENCES
NOTIFY	POINT AND COUNTRY OF ORIGIN
PIER/TERMINAL	COMBINED TRANSPORT - PLACE OF RECEIPT
VESSEL	PORT OF LOADING
PORT OF DISCHARGE	COMBINED TRANSPORT - PLACE OF DELIVERY

MARKS AND NUMBERS	NO. OF PKGS.	DESCRIPTION OF GOODS	GRS WEIGHT	MEASUREMENT

FREIGHT & CHARGES	RATE	PER	AMOUNT	PREPAID	COLLECT	LADEN ON BOARD DATE
						PLACE OF BL ISSUE
						DATE OF BL ISSUE
						BL NO.
						SIGNED BY

SHIPPER'S LOAD AND COUNT
THESE COMMODITIES, TECHNOLOGIES, OR SOFTWARE WERE EXPORTED FROM THE UNITED STATES IN ACCORDANCE WITH THE EXPORT ADMINISTRATION REGULATIONS. DIVERSION CONTRARY TO U.S. LAW IS PROHIBITED.
Received in external apparent good order and condition except as otherwise noted. The total number of the packages or units stuffed in the carrier's receipt, said to contain the goods described in the particulars furnished by the shipper to be transported to the port of discharge, or to such other place authorized or permitted herein, or so near thereto as the vessel can get, lie and leave without delay, and there to be delivered to consignee, or authorized receiver, or on carrier on payment of all charges due thereon. The description of the goods and the weights shown on this bill of lading are furnished by the merchants

JSC JOE'S SHIPPING CO. (Sample) **BILL OF LADING**

SHIPPER ABC CO., INC. 1234 A ST. ANYTOWN, USA	**BOOKING NO.** JSCU12345678 **EXPORT REFERENCES** PO#1234
CONSIGNEE BEST SPORTS, LTD. 888 OMOTE-DORI, YOKOHAMA, JAPAN	**FORWARDING AGENT REFERENCES**
NOTIFY SAME AS CONSIGNEE TEL: (XXX) XXX - XXXX FAX: (XXX) XXX - XXXX	**POINT AND COUNTRY OF ORIGIN** ANYTOWN, USA
PIER/TERMINAL	**COMBINED TRANSPORT – PLACE OF RECEIPT**
VESSEL AND VOYAGE JOE EXPRESS V. 001W	**PORT OF LOADING** LOS ANGELES
PORT OF DISCHARGE YOKOHAMA	**COMBINED TRANSPORT – PLACE OF DELIVERY**

MARKS AND NUMBERS	NO. OF PKGS.	DESCRIPTION OF GOODS	GRS WEIGHT	MEASUREMENT
"ABC CO., INC., U.S.A." CONTAINER NO. JSCU1234567 SEAL NO. 678	1000 BOXES ON 2 PALLETS	SPORTS EQUIPMENT (BASKETBALLS & VOLLEYBALLS)	204.000 KGS	2 CBM

FREIGHT & CHARGES	RATE	PER	AMOUNT	PREPAID	COLLECT	
						LADEN ON BOARD DATE JAN. 31ST 20XX
OCEAN FREIGHT	400 USD	1	400.00 USD	X		**PLACE OF BL ISSUE** LOS ANGELES
ADDL. FEES ORIGIN	100 USD	1	100.00 USD	X		**DATE OF BL ISSUE** JAN. 31ST 20XX
THC DESTINATION	5000 JPY	1	5000 JPY		X	**BL NO.** JSCU12345678
						SIGNED BY JOE E. SUCCESS

SHIPPER'S LOAD AND COUNT

THESE COMMODITIES, TECHNOLOGIES, OR SOFTWARE WERE EXPORTED FROM THE UNITED STATES IN ACCORDANCE WITH THE EXPORT ADMINISTRATION REGULATIONS. DIVERSION CONTRARY TO U.S. LAW IS PROHIBITED.

Received in external apparent good order and condition except as otherwise noted. The total number of the packages or units stuffed in the carrier's receipt, said to contain the goods described in the particulars furnished by the shipper to be transported to the port of discharge, or to such other place authorized or permitted herein, or so near thereto as the vessel can get, lie and leave without delay, and there to be delivered to consignee, or authorized receiver, or on carrier on payment of all charges due thereon. The description of the goods and the weights shown on this bill of lading are furnished by the merchants

5

Air Waybill (AWB)
Arrival Notice (A/N)
Bill of Lading (BL)

Booking Request

Cargo Insurance Certificate (COI)
Certificate of Origin (COO)
Commercial Invoice (CI)
Declaration for Free Entry of Returned U.S. Goods (USGR)
Declaration of No Wood Packing Material (WPM)
Declaration of Non-Coniferous Wood Packing Material (WPM)
Entry Summary (Customs Form 7501)
Importer Security Filing Form (ISF)
Importer's Blanket Statement of Non-Reimbursement of
Anti-Dumping Duties (AD/CVD)
Letter of Credit Application (L/C)
Packing List (PL)
Power of Attorney (POA)
Pre-Shipment Inspection Certificate (PSIC)
Pro Forma Invoice
Purchase Order (PO)
Sales Order (SO)
Shipping Instructions (SI)
Telex Release Request (TLX)
Toxic Substances Control Act Statement (TSCA)

Booking Request

ALSO KNOWN AS:
Cargo/Freight Booking Request. Cargo/Freight Pickup Request.

REQUIRED FOR:
Exports

NOT REQUIRED FOR:
N/A

ORIGINAL COPIES NORMALLY REQUIRED?:
No

IN SUMMARY:
A booking request is a request made by a shipper and addressed to a carrier for the purpose of reserving space on an upcoming vessel or flight.

USEFUL TIPS:
Securing just the right booking request can be a challenge. The following factors should be considered...

- When will the supplier have their material or shipment ready?
- By what date does the shipment need to be tendered to carrier in order to meet customer's deadline?
- Does the customer restrict the use of certain types or specific carriers?
- How many days or weeks out is the carrier booked?

WHAT TO REMEMBER:
A shipper's booking request to their carrier does not have to be a formal procedure. It can be as informal as a short email as long as all the main details pertinent to the shipment booking are effectively communicated.

Booking Request

Date:

To:

Shipper's Export Reference:
Air or Ocean:
If Ocean, Container Type:
Commodity:

Shipper:
Pickup Location:
Shipment Ready for Pickup (Date & Time):
Consignee:

Port of Loading--Door or CY:
Final Destination--Door or CY:
Special Routing Instructions?:

AES ITN#:
Hazardous Cargo?:
Ocean Freight & Origin Charges (Prepaid or Collect):
Destination Charges (Prepaid or Collect):
Cargo Insurance Required?:
Original Bills of Lading Required?:

Shipment Details:

Pallet	No. of Pkgs.	Pallet. Dims.	Grs. Wt.	Tare Wt.	Net Wt.

(Sample)

ABC Co., Inc.
1234 A St.
Anytown, USA

Booking Request

Date: 1/1/20XX

To: Joe's Shipping Co.

Shipper's Export Reference: PO#1234
Air or Ocean: Ocean
If Ocean, Container Type: Less than Container Load (LCL)
Commodity: Sports Equipment (Basketballs & Volleyballs)

Shipper: ABC Co., Inc. 1234 A St., Anytown, USA
Pickup Location: (same as above)
Shipment Ready for Pickup (Date & Time): On 01/01/20XX a.m. (8am to 12pm)
Consignee: Best Sports, Ltd. 888 Omote-Dori, Yokohama, JAPAN

Port of Loading--Door or CY: Los Angeles--Door
Final Destination--Door or CY: Yokohama--Door
Special Routing Instructions?: Please book on the vessel Joe Express v.001w

AES ITN#: Please submit AES ITN# on behalf of ABC Co., Inc.
Hazardous Cargo?: No
Ocean Freight & Origin Charges (Prepaid or Collect): All Prepaid
Destination Charges (Prepaid or Collect): All Collect
Cargo Insurance Required?: No.
Original Bills of Lading Required?: Yes.

Shipment Details:

Pallet	No. of Pkgs.	Pallet. Dims.	Grs. Wt.	Tare Wt.	Net Wt.
#1	500 Boxes	40"x40"x40"	250 Lbs	60 Lbs	190 Lbs
#2	500 Boxes	40"x40"x30"	200 Lbs	40 Lbs	160 Lbs
Totals	**1000 Boxes**	**On 2 Pallets**	**450 Lbs**	**100 Lbs**	**350 Lbs**

6

Air Waybill (AWB)
Arrival Notice (A/N)
Bill of Lading (BL)
Booking Request

Cargo Insurance Certificate (COI)

Certificate of Origin (COO)
Commercial Invoice (CI)
Declaration for Free Entry of Returned U.S. Goods (USGR)
Declaration of No Wood Packing Material (WPM)
Declaration of Non-Coniferous Wood Packing Material (WPM)
Entry Summary (Customs Form 7501)
Importer Security Filing Form (ISF)
Importer's Blanket Statement of Non-Reimbursement of
Anti-Dumping Duties (AD/CVD)
Letter of Credit Application (L/C)
Packing List (PL)
Power of Attorney (POA)
Pre-Shipment Inspection Certificate (PSIC)
Pro Forma Invoice
Purchase Order (PO)
Sales Order (SO)
Shipping Instructions (SI)
Telex Release Request (TLX)
Toxic Substances Control Act Statement (TSCA)

Cargo Insurance Certificate (COI)

ALSO KNOWN AS:
Certificate of Insurance. COI. Marine Insurance. Marine Insurance Policy.

REQUIRED FOR:
Recommended for All Imports and Exports

NOT REQUIRED FOR:
N/A

ORIGINAL COPIES NORMALLY REQUIRED?:
Yes

IN SUMMARY:
Marine insurance is like any other form of insurance in that the assured (i.e. the purchaser of the cargo insurance policy) pays a fee to the insurance/surety company in the form of a premium payment in order to protect assets (i.e. the in-transit cargo).

USEFUL TIPS:
A commonly accepted amount of coverage is 110% of the cargo value (as stated on the supplier's invoice). The average cost of coverage will vary somewhat between different insurance companies, though a rate at about 0.001 times the amount of coverage would be about average. So, for example, if an importer or exporter wanted to insure 110% of a shipment valued at $10,000.00 USD, then the amount of coverage (also known as insured value) would be $11,000.00. The cost of insurance would then be $11.00 ($11,000.00 x 0.001). Most insurance companies will allow their customers to issue their own cargo insurance certificates online via their website.

WHAT TO REMEMBER:
Generally speaking, the average marine insurance policy does not pay out under the following scenarios...

- Loss of market (i.e. a customer will not pay for the delivered goods)
- Damage or deterioration of goods arising from a prolonged shipment delay
- Loss of material due to the inherent nature of the product
- Strikes, riots, and wars (unless explicitly provided for or added to policy)

(VOID—Actual Certificate Must Be From Issuing Insurance Co.)

<table>
<tr><th colspan="2">Cargo Insurance Certificate</th></tr>
<tr><td>Insurance Company:</td><td>Date of Issuance:
Place of Issuance:
Date of Shipment:</td></tr>
<tr><td>Assured:</td><td>Policy#:
Certificate#:</td></tr>
<tr><td>Vessel/Flight:</td><td>Insured Value:</td></tr>
<tr><td>Place of Origin:</td><td>Final Destination:</td></tr>
<tr><td>Port of Loading:</td><td>Port of Discharge:</td></tr>
<tr><td colspan="2">Commodity Description:

Marks & Numbers:

Pieces & Weights:</td></tr>
<tr><td colspan="2">Notes:</td></tr>
<tr><td colspan="2">Claims Agent at Destination:</td></tr>
<tr><td colspan="2">Conditions:</td></tr>
<tr><td colspan="2">By: ______________________________ Title: ____________________ Date______________
(Signature of the Assured)</td></tr>
</table>

(Sample)

Cargo Insurance Certificate	
Insurance Company: Paco's Del Mar Marine & Casualty 1234 C St. Anytown, USA	**Date of Issuance:** 1/1/20XX **Place of Issuance:** Anytown, USA **Date of Shipment:** 1/1/20XX
Assured: ABC Co., Inc. 1234 A St., Anytown, USA	**Policy#:** 1234567 **Certificate#:** 1234567
Vessel/Flight: Joe Express v.001w	**Insured Value:** $11,000.00 USD
Place of Origin: Anytown, USA	**Final Destination:** Yokohama, Japan
Port of Loading: Los Angeles, USA	**Port of Discharge:** Yokohama, Japan
Commodity Description: Basketballs & Volleyballs **Marks & Numbers:** Container#JSCU1234567 "ABC Co, Inc., U.S.A." **Pieces & Weights:** 1000 Boxes, 450 Lbs Grs.	
Notes: Each claim for loss or damage shall include a deduction in the exact amount of the policy deductible.	
Claims Agent at Destination: Kotatsu Marine & Casualty, LLC, 234 Harbor Way, Yokohama, Japan	
Conditions: This insurance is subject to the latest American Institute Cargo Clauses Free of Particular Average—American Conditions (FPAAC) available at the time of shipment. Additional terms and conditions of this certificate available at Paco's Del Mar's homepage.	
By: ______________________________ Title: ____________________ Date____________ (Signature of the Assured)	

7

Air Waybill (AWB)
Arrival Notice (A/N)
Bill of Lading (BL)
Booking Request
Cargo Insurance Certificate (COI)

Certificate of Origin (COO)

Commercial Invoice (CI)
Declaration for Free Entry of Returned U.S. Goods (USGR)
Declaration of No Wood Packing Material (WPM)
Declaration of Non-Coniferous Wood Packing Material (WPM)
Entry Summary (Customs Form 7501)
Importer Security Filing Form (ISF)
Importer's Blanket Statement of Non-Reimbursement of
Anti-Dumping Duties (AD/CVD)
Letter of Credit Application (L/C)
Packing List (PL)
Power of Attorney (POA)
Pre-Shipment Inspection Certificate (PSIC)
Pro Forma Invoice
Purchase Order (PO)
Sales Order (SO)
Shipping Instructions (SI)
Telex Release Request (TLX)
Toxic Substances Control Act Statement (TSCA)

Certificate of Origin (COO)

ALSO KNOWN AS:
COO.

REQUIRED FOR:
Some Imports and Exports

NOT REQUIRED FOR:
N/A

ORIGINAL COPIES NORMALLY REQUIRED?:
No

IN SUMMARY:
Although the commercial invoice will also usually contain a statement regarding the country of origin of the goods, the certificate of origin is a separate document by which the shipper or manufacturer certifies that the goods contained herein are products of their country. A local chamber of commerce can also separately provide a certificate of origin, and if required, a certificate of origin may also be notarized.

USEFUL TIPS:
In general, if a product consists of material or parts from more than one country, then the country of origin of the commodity is the material or part that imparts the essential character of the good. For example, if all the parts of a child's bicycle were produced in the USA except for the training wheels, then the finished product would still be considered as originating in the USA. For specific advice on this topic concerning your product, you may consult with your customs broker.

WHAT TO REMEMBER:
A certificate of origin may be required depending on the customer, country of import, and type of commodity. When in doubt whether a certificate of origin is required or not for your shipment, go ahead and include it with the rest of your documents.

Certificate of Origin

Date:
Certificate#:
Invoice#:

Sold To:
Ship To:

Name of Person Completing Certificate:
Name of Firm:
Actual Mfr:

Carrier:

Qty.	Unit	No. Pkg.	Grs. Wt.	Tare Wt.	Net Wt.	Description of Goods

Marks: "ABC Co., Inc., U.S.A."

I declare that I am the person named above, acting in the capacity indicated, that the description and other particulars of the merchandise as specified above are correct as set forth in this certificate, and that the said merchandise was produced or manufactured in the United States of America.

By: ______________________________ Title: ____________________
(signature)

(Sample)

ABC Co., Inc.
1234 A St.
Anytown, USA

Certificate of Origin

Date: 1/1/20XX
Certificate#: 1234ABC
Invoice#: 1234

Sold To: Best Sports, Ltd. 888 Omote-Dori, Yokohama, JAPAN
Ship To: (same as above)

Name of Person Completing Certificate: Jane Doe
Name of Firm: ABC Co., Inc.
Actual Mfr: ABC Co., Inc.

Carrier: Hyundai Merchant Marine

Qty.	Unit	No. Pkg.	Grs. Wt.	Tare Wt.	Net Wt.	Description of Goods
500	Each	500 Boxes	0.5 Lbs	0.1 Lbs	0.4 Lbs	Basketballs (rubber)
500	Each	500 Boxes	0.4 Lbs	0.1 Lbs	0.3 Lbs	Volleyballs (synth. leather)
		1000 Boxes	**450 Lbs**	**100 Lbs**	**350 Lbs**	**Packaging Totals**

Marks: "ABC Co., Inc., U.S.A."

I declare that I am the person named above, acting in the capacity indicated, that the description and other particulars of the merchandise as specified above are correct as set forth in this certificate, and that the said merchandise was produced or manufactured in the United States of America.

By: ______________________________ Title: ____________________
(signature)

8

Air Waybill (AWB)
Arrival Notice (A/N)
Bill of Lading (BL)
Booking Request
Cargo Insurance Certificate (COI)
Certificate of Origin (COO)

Commercial Invoice (CI)

Declaration for Free Entry of Returned U.S. Goods (USGR)
Declaration of No Wood Packing Material (WPM)
Declaration of Non-Coniferous Wood Packing Material (WPM)
Entry Summary (Customs Form 7501)
Importer Security Filing Form (ISF)
Importer's Blanket Statement of Non-Reimbursement of
Anti-Dumping Duties (AD/CVD)
Letter of Credit Application (L/C)
Packing List (PL)
Power of Attorney (POA)
Pre-Shipment Inspection Certificate (PSIC)
Pro Forma Invoice
Purchase Order (PO)
Sales Order (SO)
Shipping Instructions (SI)
Telex Release Request (TLX)
Toxic Substances Control Act Statement (TSCA)

Commercial Invoice (CI)

ALSO KNOWN AS:
CI. Invoice. Customs Invoice.

REQUIRED FOR:
All Imports and Exports

NOT REQUIRED FOR:
N/A

ORIGINAL COPIES NORMALLY REQUIRED?:
No

IN SUMMARY:
The commercial invoice officially documents the details of a business transaction between two parties, and is used by customs to accurately assess the true value of the shipment.

USEFUL TIPS:
Remember the acronym "PIT CAR FUD" as a reminder for the most important elements to include on the commercial invoice to help ensure trouble-free customs clearances.

P = Pieces (quantity and unit of measure)
I = Importer of Record (sold to party)
T = Terms of Sale (INCO Terms)
C = Country of Origin (country where the goods were produced)
A = Actual Manufacturer (name and address--if known)
R = Related Parties? (shipper and importer)
F = Freight Charges (estimated ocean or air freight charges)
U = USD (Currency)
D = Description (in as much detail as possible)

WHAT TO REMEMBER:
Additional information may be added to the commercial invoice, including but not limited to: purchase order number, letter of credit number, container and seal number, carrier vessel or flight details, estimated departure and arrival dates, harmonized tariff schedule number, as well as any other information pertinent to the order or shipment.

Commercial Invoice

Date:
Invoice#:

Sold To:
Ship To:

Terms of Sale:
Country of Origin and Export:
Actual Mfr:
Freight Charges:

Qty.	Unit of Measure	Unit Price	Description of Goods	Total Value (USD)
			Total	

I certify that these goods are of USA origin, and this invoice to be true and correct.

By: ______________________________ Title: ____________________

(signature)

(Sample)

ABC Co., Inc.
1234 A St.
Anytown, USA

Commercial Invoice

Date: 1/1/20XX
Invoice#: 1234

Sold To: Best Sports, Ltd. 888 Omote-Dori, Yokohama, JAPAN
Ship To: (same as above)

Terms of Sale: C&F Yokohama
Country of Origin and Export: USA
Actual Mfr: ABC Co., Inc.
Freight Charges: $500.00 USD

Qty.	Unit of Measure	Unit Price	Description of Goods	Total Value (USD)
500	Each	10.00	Basketballs (rubber)	$5,000.00
500	Each	10.00	Volleyballs (synth. leather)	$5,000.00
			Total	**$10,000.00**

I certify that these goods are of USA origin, and this invoice to be true and correct.

By: ______________________________ Title: ____________________
(signature)

9

Air Waybill (AWB)
Arrival Notice (A/N)
Bill of Lading (BL)
Booking Request
Cargo Insurance Certificate (COI)
Certificate of Origin (COO)
Commercial Invoice (CI)

Declaration for Free Entry of Returned U.S. Goods (USGR)

Declaration of No Wood Packing Material (WPM)
Declaration of Non-Coniferous Wood Packing Material (WPM)
Entry Summary (Customs Form 7501)
Importer Security Filing Form (ISF)
Importer's Blanket Statement of Non-Reimbursement of
Anti-Dumping Duties (AD/CVD)
Letter of Credit Application (L/C)
Packing List (PL)
Power of Attorney (POA)
Pre-Shipment Inspection Certificate (PSIC)
Pro Forma Invoice
Purchase Order (PO)
Sales Order (SO)
Shipping Instructions (SI)
Telex Release Request (TLX)
Toxic Substances Control Act Statement (TSCA)

Declaration for Free Entry of Returned U.S. Goods (USGR)

ALSO KNOWN AS:
USGR. U.S./American Goods Returned Declaration. AGR.

REQUIRED FOR:
Duty exemption for Imports that are of U.S. origin and being shipped back to the U.S.

NOT REQUIRED FOR:
N/A

ORIGINAL COPIES NORMALLY REQUIRED?:
No

IN SUMMARY:
The "declaration for free entry of returned U.S. goods" is an affidavit made by both the shipper and the importer stating that their imported product is of U.S. origin and has not been advanced in value abroad in order to allow it duty free entry to the United States.

USEFUL TIPS:
Per the United States Code of Federal Regulations, Title 19 (Customs Duties), in any case in which the value of the returned articles exceeds $2,500 and the articles are not clearly marked with the name and address of the U.S. manufacturer, the port director may require, in addition to the declaration, such as a statement from the U.S. manufacturer verifying that the articles were made in the U.S., a U.S. export invoice, bill of lading or airway bill evidencing the U.S. origin of the articles and/or the reason for the exportation of the articles.

WHAT TO REMEMBER:
Per the United States Code of Federal Regulations, Title 19 (Customs Duties), the declaration must be made by the owner, importer, consignee, or agent having knowledge of the facts regarding the claim for free entry. If the owner or ultimate consignee is a corporation, such declaration may be signed by the president, vice president, secretary, or treasurer of the corporation, or may be signed by any employee or agent of the corporation who holds a power of attorney and a certification by the corporation that such employee or other agent has or will have knowledge of the pertinent facts.

Declaration for Free Entry of Returned U.S. Goods

Shipper's Declaration:

I, ________________ (printed name), declare that to the best of my knowledge and belief that the articles herein specified were exported from the United States, from the port of _________ on or about _________, 20__, and that they are returned without having been advanced in value or improved in condition by any process of manufacture or other means.

Marks	Number	Quantity	Description	Value, USD

Date: ____

Address: ____

Signature: ____

Capacity: ____

Importer's Declaration:

I, ________________________ (printed name), declare that the (above) declaration by the foreign shipper is true and correct to the best of my knowledge and belief, that the articles were manufactured by _________________ (name of manufacturer) located in ________________________ (city and state), that the articles were not manufactured or produced in the United States under subheading 9813.00.05, HTSUS, and that the articles were exported from the United States without benefit of drawback.

Date: ____

Address: ____

Signature: ____

Capacity: ____

(Sample)

Declaration for Free Entry of Returned U.S. Goods

Shipper's Declaration:

I, _Deng Xiaoping__ (printed name), declare that to the best of my knowledge and belief that the articles herein specified were exported from the United States, from the port of _Seattle_ on or about _Jan. 1st__, 20XX, and that they are returned without having been advanced in value or improved in condition by any process of manufacture or other means.

Marks	Number	Quantity	Description	Value, USD

Date: ______________________________

Address: ______________________________

Signature: ______________________________

Capacity: ______________________________

Importer's Declaration:

I, _Howard Hughes__________ (printed name), declare that the (above) declaration by the foreign shipper is true and correct to the best of my knowledge and belief, that the articles were manufactured by _The Boeing Co.___ (name of manufacturer) located in _Seattle, WA_____________ (city and state), that the articles were not manufactured or produced in the United States under subheading 9813.00.05, HTSUS, and that the articles were exported from the United States without benefit of drawback.

Date: ______________________________

Address: ______________________________

Signature: ______________________________

Capacity: ______________________________

10

Air Waybill (AWB)
Arrival Notice (A/N)
Bill of Lading (BL)
Booking Request
Cargo Insurance Certificate (COI)
Certificate of Origin (COO)
Commercial Invoice (CI)
Declaration for Free Entry of Returned U.S. Goods (USGR)

Declaration of No Wood Packing Material (WPM)

Declaration of Non-Coniferous Wood Packing Material (WPM)
Entry Summary (Customs Form 7501)
Importer Security Filing Form (ISF)
Importer's Blanket Statement of Non-Reimbursement of
Anti-Dumping Duties (AD/CVD)
Letter of Credit Application (L/C)
Packing List (PL)
Power of Attorney (POA)
Pre-Shipment Inspection Certificate (PSIC)
Pro Forma Invoice
Purchase Order (PO)
Sales Order (SO)
Shipping Instructions (SI)
Telex Release Request (TLX)
Toxic Substances Control Act Statement (TSCA)

Declaration of No Wood Packing Material (WPM)

ALSO KNOWN OR REFERRED TO AS:
No (Solid) Wood Packing Material Certificate/Statement. WPM. ISPM 15.

REQUIRED FOR:
Exports to China, for which the shipper wants to certify, do not contain any solid wood packing material such as crates, pallets, etc.

NOT REQUIRED FOR:
N/A

ORIGINAL COPIES NORMALLY REQUIRED?:
No

IN SUMMARY:
Most countries require all imported solid (i.e. raw and unprocessed) wood packing material (WPM) to be either heat treated or fumigated, and subsequently stamped certifying this.

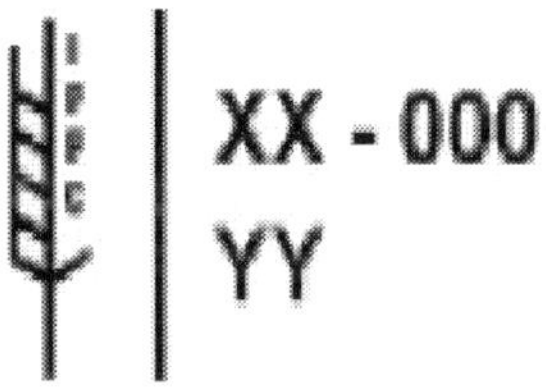

XX = Country of manufacture:
000 = Code traceable to the source (pallet manufacturer)
YY = Treatment Measure (HT or MB [fumigated])

In addition to this requirement, the China customs service requires documentation of at least one of the following...

- Declaration of no wood packing material
- Declaration of non-coniferous wood packing material
- Certificate of fumigation
- Certificate of heat treatment

USEFUL TIPS:
Information regarding both heat and fumigation treatment and certification of the same can be found on USDA's website...

http://www.aphis.usda.gov/import_export/plants/plant_exports/wpm/index.shtml

Declaration of No Wood Packing Material

To the services of China Entry & Exit Inspection and Quarantine: It is advised that this shipment does not contain any solid wood packing material.

Shipment# (BL#, AWB#, or Booking#):
Country of Origin and Export:

Qty.	Unit	No. Pkg.	Pkg. Dims.	Grs. Wt.	Tare Wt.	Net Wt.	Description of Goods
							Packaging Totals

Marks:

By: ______________________________ Title: ____________________ Date_____________
(Exporter's signature)

(Sample)

ABC Co., Inc.
1234 A St.
Anytown, USA

Declaration of No Wood Packing Material

To the services of China Entry & Exit Inspection and Quarantine: It is advised that this shipment does not contain any solid wood packing material.

Shipment# (BL#, AWB#, or Booking#): BL# JSCU12345678
Country of Origin and Export: USA

Qty.	Unit	No. Pkg.	Pkg. Dims.	Grs. Wt.	Tare Wt.	Net Wt.	Description of Goods
500	Each	500 Boxes	7"x7"x7" (per box)	0.5 Lbs	0.1 Lbs	0.4 Lbs	Basketballs (rubber)
500	Each	500 Boxes	5"x5"x5" (per box)	0.4 Lbs	0.1 Lbs	0.3 Lbs	Volleyballs (synth. leather)
		1000 Boxes	**(cardboard)**	**450 Lbs**	**100 Lbs**	**350 Lbs**	**Packaging Totals**

Marks: "ABC Co., Inc., U.S.A."

By: ______________________________ Title: ____________________ Date______________
(Exporter's signature)

11

Air Waybill (AWB)
Arrival Notice (A/N)
Bill of Lading (BL)
Booking Request
Cargo Insurance Certificate (COI)
Certificate of Origin (COO)
Commercial Invoice (CI)
Declaration for Free Entry of Returned U.S. Goods (USGR)
Declaration of No Wood Packing Material (WPM)

Declaration of Non-Coniferous Wood Packing Material (WPM)

Entry Summary (Customs Form 7501)
Importer Security Filing Form (ISF)
Importer's Blanket Statement of Non-Reimbursement of
Anti-Dumping Duties (AD/CVD)
Letter of Credit Application (L/C)
Packing List (PL)
Power of Attorney (POA)
Pre-Shipment Inspection Certificate (PSIC)
Pro Forma Invoice
Purchase Order (PO)
Sales Order (SO)
Shipping Instructions (SI)
Telex Release Request (TLX)
Toxic Substances Control Act Statement (TSCA)

Declaration of Non-Coniferous Wood Packing Material (WPM)

ALSO KNOWN OR REFERRED TO AS:
Non-Coniferous Wood Packing Material Certificate/Statement. WPM. ISPM 15.

REQUIRED FOR:
Exports to China, for which the shipper wants to certify, do not contain any coniferous wood packing material such as crates, pallets, etc.

NOT REQUIRED FOR:
N/A

ORIGINAL COPIES NORMALLY REQUIRED?:
No

IN SUMMARY:
Most countries require all imported solid (i.e. raw and unprocessed) wood packing material (WPM) to be either heat treated or fumigated, and subsequently stamped certifying this.

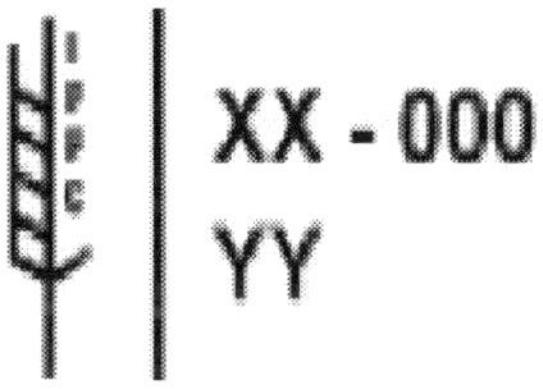

XX = Country of manufacture:
000 = Code traceable to the source (pallet manufacturer)
YY = Treatment Measure (HT or MB [fumigated])

In addition to this requirement, the China customs service requires documentation of at least one of the following...

- Declaration of no wood packing material
- Declaration of non-coniferous wood packing material
- Certificate of fumigation
- Certificate of heat treatment

USEFUL TIPS:
Information regarding both heat and fumigation treatment and certification of the same can be found on USDA's website...

http://www.aphis.usda.gov/import_export/plants/plant_exports/wpm/index.shtml

Declaration of Non-Coniferous Wood Packing Material

To the services of China Entry & Exit Inspection and Quarantine: It is advised that all wood packing materials in this shipment are made of non-coniferous trees.

Shipment# (BL#, AWB#, or Booking#):
Country of Origin and Export:

Qty.	Unit	No. Pkg.	Pkg. Dims.	Grs. Wt.	Tare Wt.	Net Wt.	Description of Goods
							Packaging Totals

Marks:

By: ______________________________ Title: ____________________ Date_____________
(Exporter's signature)

(Sample)

ABC Co., Inc.
1234 A St.
Anytown, USA

Declaration of Non-Coniferous Wood Packing Material

To the services of China Entry & Exit Inspection and Quarantine: It is advised that all wood packing materials in this shipment are made of non-coniferous trees.

Shipment# (BL#, AWB#, or Booking#): BL# JSCU12345678
Country of Origin and Export: USA

Qty.	Unit	No. Pkg.	Pkg. Dims.	Grs. Wt.	Tare Wt.	Net Wt.	Description of Goods
500	Each	500 Boxes	7"x7"x7" (per box)	0.5 Lbs	0.1 Lbs	0.4 Lbs	Basketballs (rubber)
500	Each	500 Boxes	5"x5"x5" (per box)	0.4 Lbs	0.1 Lbs	0.3 Lbs	Volleyballs (synth. leather)
		1000 Boxes	**(cardboard)**	**450 Lbs**	**100 Lbs**	**350 Lbs**	**Packaging Totals**

Marks: "ABC Co., Inc., U.S.A."

By: ______________________________ Title: ____________________ Date____________

(Exporter's signature)

12

Air Waybill (AWB)
Arrival Notice (A/N)
Bill of Lading (BL)
Booking Request
Cargo Insurance Certificate (COI)
Certificate of Origin (COO)
Commercial Invoice (CI)
Declaration for Free Entry of Returned U.S. Goods (USGR)
Declaration of No Wood Packing Material (WPM)
Declaration of Non-Coniferous Wood Packing Material (WPM)

Entry Summary (Customs Form 7501)

Importer Security Filing Form (ISF)
Importer's Blanket Statement of Non-Reimbursement of
Anti-Dumping Duties (AD/CVD)
Letter of Credit Application (L/C)
Packing List (PL)
Power of Attorney (POA)
Pre-Shipment Inspection Certificate (PSIC)
Pro Forma Invoice
Purchase Order (PO)
Sales Order (SO)
Shipping Instructions (SI)
Telex Release Request (TLX)
Toxic Substances Control Act Statement (TSCA)

Entry Summary (Customs Form 7501)

ALSO KNOWN AS:
7501. CBP FORM 7501.

REQUIRED FOR:
Most U.S. Imports

NOT REQUIRED FOR:
Exports

ORIGINAL COPIES NORMALLY REQUIRED?:
No

IN SUMMARY:
The entry summary is just as its name suggests. It is a final detailed summary whereby the importer (or customs broker on importer's behalf) provides to U.S. Customs all of the details of their importation, including harmonized tariff schedule (HTSUS) classification, value of shipment, special program indicator (SPI) for the sake of duty reduction such as NAFTA, etc. if applicable, the resulting duties, as well as other necessary statistical information,

USEFUL TIPS:
The completion and filing of the importer's entry summary to Customs can be likened to the filing of an individual's income taxes to the IRS. On the entry summary, the importer makes truthful and well-informed declarations regarding classification, valuation, and possible duty exempt status of their shipment. U.S. Customs depends on the accuracy of this information in order to effectively collect duties and taxes. And, just as a certified public accountant (CPA) can complete IRS form 1040, etc. on behalf of a taxpayer, a licensed customs broker (LCB) can complete, compute, and file the Customs form 7501 as a service for the importer. Instructions for filling out this Customs form as well as other downloadable Customs forms can be found on Customs' website.

http://www.cbp.gov/xp/cgov/toolbox/forms/

WHAT TO REMEMBER:
Though most U.S. imports are granted conditional releases soon after the importer or customs broker submits an entry to Customs, the "entry summary" along with payment of estimated duties must be filed within 10 working days of the shipment's release date.

Form Approved OMB No. 1651-0022
EXP. 08-31-2014

DEPARTMENT OF HOMELAND SECURITY
U.S. Customs and Border Protection

ENTRY SUMMARY

1. Filer Code/Entry No.		2. Entry Type	3. Summary Date
4. Surety No.	5. Bond Type	6. Port Code	7. Entry Date

8. Importing Carrier	9. Mode of Transport	10. Country of Origin	11. Import Date
12. B/L or AWB No.	13. Manufacturer ID	14. Exporting Country	15. Export Date

16. I.T. No.	17. I.T. Date	18. Missing Docs	19. Foreign Port of Lading	20. U.S. Port of Unlading

21. Location of Goods/G.O. No.	22. Consignee No.	23. Importer No.	24. Reference No.

25. Ultimate Consignee Name and Address	26. Importer of Record Name and Address
City State Zip	City State Zip

27. Line No.	28. Description of Merchandise: 29. A. HTSUS No. B. ADA/CVD No.	30. A. Grossweight B. Manifest Qty.	31. Net Quantity in HTSUS Units	32. A. Entered Value B. CHGS C. Relationship	33. A. HTSUS Rate B. ADA/CVD Rate C. IRC Rate D. Visa No.	34. Duty and I.R. Tax: Dollars Cents

Other Fee Summary for Block 39	35. Total Entered Value $		
	Total Other Fees $		

CBP USE ONLY

A. LIQ CODE	B. Ascertained Duty	**TOTALS** 37. Duty
REASON CODE	C. Ascertained Tax	38. Tax
	D. Ascertained Other	39. Other
	E. Ascertained Total	40. Total

36. DECLARATION OF IMPORTER OF RECORD (OWNER OR PURCHASER) OR AUTHORIZED AGENT

I declare that I am the ☐ Importer of record and that the actual owner, purchaser, or consignee for CBP purposes is as shown above, **OR** ☐ owner or purchaser or agent thereof. I further declare that the merchandise ☐ was obtained pursuant to a purchase or agreement to purchase and that the prices set forth in the invoices are true, **OR** ☐ was not obtained pursuant to a purchase or agreement to purchase and the statements in the invoices as to value or price are true to the best of my knowledge and belief. I also declare that the statements in the documents herein filed fully disclose to the best of my knowledge and belief the true prices, values, quantities, rebates, drawbacks, fees, commissions, and royalties and are true and correct, and that all goods or services provided to the seller of the merchandise either free or at reduced cost are fully disclosed.
I will immediately furnish to the appropriate CBP officer any information showing a different statement of facts.

41. DECLARANT NAME	TITLE	SIGNATURE	DATE

42. Broker/Filer Information (Name, address, phone number)	43. Broker/Importer File No.

CBP Form 7501 (06/09)

Form Approved OMB No. 1651-0022
EXP. 08-31-2014

DEPARTMENT OF HOMELAND SECURITY
U.S. Customs and Border Protection

ENTRY SUMMARY

1. Filer Code/Entry No. AAA-XXXXXXX-X	2. Entry Type 01 ABI/A	3. Summary Date 01/09/2013	
4. Surety No. XXX	5. Bond Type 8	6. Port Code 2704	7. Entry Date 01/01/2013

8. Importing Carrier JOE EXPRESS V.002E	9. Mode of Transport 10	10. Country of Origin JP	11. Import Date 01/01/2013
12. B/L or AWB No. JSCU12345678	13. Manufacturer ID JPBESSPO888YOK	14. Exporting Country JP	15. Export Date 12/21/2012
16. I.T. No. / 17. I.T. Date / 18. Missing Docs		19. Foreign Port of Lading 58895	20. U.S. Port of Unlading 2704
21. Location of Goods/G.O. No. AXXX	22. Consignee No. XX-XXXXXXX	23. Importer No. XX-XXXXXXX	24. Reference No.

25. Ultimate Consignee Name and Address
City State CA Zip

26. Importer of Record Name and Address
ABC CO., INC.
1234 A ST.
City ANYTOWN State CA Zip XXXXX

27. Line No.	28. Description of Merchandise (29. A. HTSUS No. B. ADA/CVD No.; 30. A. Grossweight B. Manifest Qty.; 31. Net Quantity in HTSUS Units)	32. A. Entered Value B. CHGS C. Relationship	33. A. HTSUS Rate B. ADA/CVD Rate C. IRC Rate D. Visa No.	34. Duty and I.R. Tax (Dollars / Cents)
	150 KGS. 1000 BOXES BL#JSCU23456789	NOT RELATED		
001	BASEBALLS HTSUS 9506.69.2040 150 KGS. 1000 NO.	5000 C 500	FREE	0.00
	HARBOR MAINTENANCE FEE		0.125%	6.25
	MERCHANDISE PROCESSING FEE		0.3464%	17.32
	ENTERED VALUE USD 5000			

Other Fee Summary for Block 39 501 6.25 499 25.00	35. Total Entered Value $ 5,000.00 Total Other Fees $ 31.25	**CBP USE ONLY** A. LIQ CODE REASON CODE	B. Ascertained Duty C. Ascertained Tax D. Ascertained Other E. Ascertained Total	TOTALS 37. Duty 0.00 38. Tax 0.00 39. Other 31.25 40. Total 31.25

36. DECLARATION OF IMPORTER OF RECORD (OWNER OR PURCHASER) OR AUTHORIZED AGENT

I declare that I am the ☐ Importer of record and that the actual owner, purchaser, or consignee for CBP purposes is as shown above, **OR** ☒ owner or purchaser or agent thereof. I further declare that the merchandise ☒ was obtained pursuant to a purchase or agreement to purchase and that the prices set forth in the invoices are true, **OR** ☐ was not obtained pursuant to a purchase or agreement to purchase and the statements in the invoices as to value or price are true to the best of my knowledge and belief. I also declare that the statements in the documents herein filed fully disclose to the best of my knowledge and belief the true prices, values, quantities, rebates, drawbacks, fees, commissions, and royalties and are true and correct, and that all goods or services provided to the seller of the merchandise either free or at reduced cost are fully disclosed.
I will immediately furnish to the appropriate CBP officer any information showing a different statement of facts.

41. DECLARANT NAME	TITLE	SIGNATURE	DATE
DAVE THOMAS	ATTY-IN-FACT		01/01/2013

42. Broker/Filer Information (Name, address, phone number)
PERFECT CUSTOMS BROKERAGE, INC.
888 CIRCULAR DR., ANYTOWN, USA
TEL: (XXX)XXX-XXXX

43. Broker/Importer File No.
12345

CBP Form 7501 (06/09)

13

Air Waybill (AWB)
Arrival Notice (A/N)
Bill of Lading (BL)
Booking Request
Cargo Insurance Certificate (COI)
Certificate of Origin (COO)
Commercial Invoice (CI)
Declaration for Free Entry of Returned U.S. Goods (USGR)
Declaration of No Wood Packing Material (WPM)
Declaration of Non-Coniferous Wood Packing Material (WPM)
Entry Summary (Customs Form 7501)

Importer Security Filing Form (ISF)

Importer's Blanket Statement of Non-Reimbursement of
Anti-Dumping Duties (AD/CVD)
Letter of Credit Application (L/C)
Packing List (PL)
Power of Attorney (POA)
Pre-Shipment Inspection Certificate (PSIC)
Pro Forma Invoice
Purchase Order (PO)
Sales Order (SO)
Shipping Instructions (SI)
Telex Release Request (TLX)
Toxic Substances Control Act Statement (TSCA)

Importer Security Filing (ISF)

ALSO KNOWN AS:
ISF. 10 + 2.

REQUIRED FOR:
All containerized and break bulk ocean Imports (destined for the United States).

NOT REQUIRED FOR:
Air Imports or Exports

ORIGINAL COPIES NORMALLY REQUIRED?:
No

IN SUMMARY:
For national security purposes, US Customs and Border Protection (CBP) absolutely requires importers (or their agents on their behalf) to submit electronically to CBP, at least 24 - 48 hours prior to their shipment being loaded on a U.S. destined vessel, 10 specific data sets of their cargo. They include...

1) Importer of record ID# (IRS# or Customs ID#)
2) Consignee ID#
3) Buyer name and address
4) Ship-to location name and address
5) Seller name and address
6) Manufacturer (or supplier) name and address
7) Container stuffing location name and address
8) Container consolidator (stuffer) name and address
9) Country of origin
10) Harmonized Tariff Schedule (HTS) number/code (at least up to six-digit level)

USEFUL TIPS:
Importer compliance with ISF requirements is highly dependant on an open line of communication between the shipper (seller) and importer (buyer). The foreign seller must be well aware at the time of the order that they are obligated to furnish the buyer with the required ISF data elements in order to avoid costly US Customs penalties.

WHAT TO REMEMBER:
Whether the importer transmits their ISF by themselves or through the services of a freight forwarder or customs broker, the transmission of ISF information must at least be 24 - 48 hours prior to the loading of the ocean container onto the vessel. Non-compliance penalties can be as much as $5,000.00 USD per violation.

Importer Security Filing Form (ISF)

To:

Master BOL#:
House BOL# (if applicable):
Estimated Load Date:

Importer of Record (IOR):
IOR ID#:
Consignee ID#:
Buyer:
Ship To:

Seller Name & Address:
Manufacturer Name & Address:
Container Stuffing Name & Address:
Consolidator Name & Address:

Description of Goods	Country of Origin	Harmonized Code (HTS)

By: ______________________________ Title: ____________________ Date____________

(Importer's signature)

(Sample)

ABC Co., Inc.
1234 A St.
Anytown, USA

Importer Security Filing Form (ISF)

To: Perfect Customs Brokerage, Inc.

Master BOL#: JSCU23456789
House BOL# (if applicable): N/A
Estimated Load Date: 12/21/20XX

Importer of Record (IOR): ABC Co., Inc. 1234 A St. Anytown, USA
IOR ID#: XX-XXXXXXX
Consignee ID#: (same as above)
Buyer: (same as above)
Ship To: (same as above)

Seller Name & Address: Best Sports, Ltd. 888 Omote-Dori, Yokohama, JAPAN
Manufacturer Name & Address: (same as above)
Container Stuffing Name & Address: (same as above)
Consolidator Name & Address: (same as above)

Description of Goods	Country of Origin	Harmonized Code (HTS)
Baseballs (leather)	Japan	9506.69.2040
Soccer balls (rubber)	Japan	9506.62.4080

By: ______________________________ Title: ____________________ Date______________
(Importer's signature)

14

Air Waybill (AWB)
Arrival Notice (A/N)
Bill of Lading (BL)
Booking Request
Cargo Insurance Certificate (COI)
Certificate of Origin (COO)
Commercial Invoice (CI)
Declaration for Free Entry of Returned U.S. Goods (USGR)
Declaration of No Wood Packing Material (WPM)
Declaration of Non-Coniferous Wood Packing Material (WPM)
Entry Summary (Customs Form 7501)
Importer Security Filing Form (ISF)

Importer's Blanket Statement of Non-Reimbursement of Anti-Dumping Duties (AD/CVD)

Letter of Credit Application (L/C)
Packing List (PL)
Power of Attorney (POA)
Pre-Shipment Inspection Certificate (PSIC)
Pro Forma Invoice
Purchase Order (PO)
Sales Order (SO)
Shipping Instructions (SI)
Telex Release Request (TLX)
Toxic Substances Control Act Statement (TSCA)

Importer's Blanket Statement of Non-Reimbursement of Anti-Dumping Duties (AD/CVD)

ALSO KNOWN AS:
Blanket Statement/Certificate. Non-Reimbursement Statement/Certificate.

REQUIRED FOR:
Imports that contain a commodity that is subject to anti-dumping duties.

NOT REQUIRED FOR:
N/A

ORIGINAL COPIES NORMALLY REQUIRED?:
No

IN SUMMARY:
The "importer's blanket statement of non-reimbursement of anti-dumping duties" is essentially an affidavit signed by the importer of record stating that their supplier (i.e. the shipper) will not reimburse them for anti-dumping duties payable by the importer to U.S. Customs. The statement references a specific commodity and a defined period of time. Anti-dumping cases are determined by the U.S. government in response to country-specific imports deemed sold to U.S. importers at a price significantly lower than in the foreign/home country.

USEFUL TIPS:
A sample of U.S. initiated anti-dumping cases is as follows...

- Steel and steel products from various countries
- Polyethylene retail carrier bags various countries
- Various products from China (cased pencils, fresh garlic, steel nails, etc.)
- Pasta from Italy
- Certain lined paper from India

WHAT TO REMEMBER:
Go to www.usitc.gov and see a list of current antidumping cases on the U.S. International Trade Commission's (USITC) website.

Importer's Blanket Statement of Non-Reimbursement of Anti-Dumping Duties

Date:
Importer:
Manufacturer:
Anti-Dumping Case Number:

I hereby certify that I have not entered into any agreement or understanding for the payment or for the reimbursement to me, by the manufacturer, producer, seller or exporter of all or any part of the antidumping duties upon all shipments of:

Commodity: ____

Countries of Origin: ____

Which have been and/or will be imported by this company.

This blanket applies to importations from (date): ______________to (date):______________
I further certify that the U.S. Customs and Border Protection will be notified if there is any reimbursement of antidumping duties by the manufacturer, producer, seller, or exporter to the importing company at any time in the future.

Information regarding any refund of antidumping duties must be sent immediately to the CBP Port Director where this certificate is filed.

Failure to file this certificate prior to liquidation will result in the presumption of reimbursement and the assessment of double the antidumping duties.

By: ______________________________ Title: ____________________
(signature of company officer)

(Sample)

ABC Co., Inc.
1234 A St.
Anytown, USA

Importer's Blanket Statement of Non-Reimbursement of Anti-Dumping Duties

Date: 1/1/20XX
Importer: ABC Co., Inc.
Manufacturer: Best Sports, Ltd. 888 Omote-Dori, Yokohama, JAPAN
Anti-Dumping Case Number: AXXX-XXX-XXX

I hereby certify that I have not entered into any agreement or understanding for the payment or for the reimbursement to me, by the manufacturer, producer, seller or exporter of all or any part of the antidumping duties upon all shipments of:

Commodity: ___Steel Ball Bearings______________________________

Countries of Origin: _____Japan______________________________

Which have been and/or will be imported by this company.

This blanket applies to importations from (date): _1/1/20XX_____to (date):_1/1/20XX __
I further certify that the U.S. Customs and Border Protection will be notified if there is any reimbursement of antidumping duties by the manufacturer, producer, seller, or exporter to the importing company at any time in the future.

Information regarding any refund of antidumping duties must be sent immediately to the CBP Port Director where this certificate is filed.

Failure to file this certificate prior to liquidation will result in the presumption of reimbursement and the assessment of double the antidumping duties.

By: ______________________________ Title: ____________________
(signature of company officer)

15

Air Waybill (AWB)
Arrival Notice (A/N)
Bill of Lading (BL)
Booking Request
Cargo Insurance Certificate (COI)
Certificate of Origin (COO)
Commercial Invoice (CI)
Declaration for Free Entry of Returned U.S. Goods (USGR)
Declaration of No Wood Packing Material (WPM)
Declaration of Non-Coniferous Wood Packing Material (WPM)
Entry Summary (Customs Form 7501)
Importer Security Filing Form (ISF)
Importer's Blanket Statement of Non-Reimbursement of
Anti-Dumping Duties (AD/CVD)

Letter of Credit Application (L/C)

Packing List (PL)
Power of Attorney (POA)
Pre-Shipment Inspection Certificate (PSIC)
Pro Forma Invoice
Purchase Order (PO)
Sales Order (SO)
Shipping Instructions (SI)
Telex Release Request (TLX)
Toxic Substances Control Act Statement (TSCA)

Letter of Credit Application (L/C)

ALSO KNOWN AS:
Request to Open L/C. Application for Documentary Letter of Credit.

REQUIRED FOR:
Imports or Exports for which the agreed-upon form of payment is via a letter of credit

NOT REQUIRED FOR:
N/A

ORIGINAL COPIES NORMALLY REQUIRED?:
No

IN SUMMARY:
A letter of credit is a widely used international trade instrument of payment whereby the importer's bank pays the exporter subject to the exporter shipping the order and subsequently providing shipping documents exactly as per the terms and conditions as specified on the letter of credit.

USEFUL TIPS:
Most letters of credit are of the type called "irrevocable letter of credit", which means that the importer/buyer cannot unilaterally revise or cancel the letter of credit without the consent of both the importer/buyer and the exporter/supplier. This form of the L/C is more expensive than the "revocable letter of credit", however, it helps to ensure that the exporter is rightfully paid assuming he or she adheres to the terms and conditions of the "irrevocable letter of credit".

WHAT TO REMEMBER:
Correct spelling (even misspellings) and punctuation on shipping documents should match verbatim as spelled out on the letter of credit. Any such discrepancies could result in non-payment or in a delay of payment. The following documents are usually included in the list of required documents as advised by the L/C issuing bank.

- Bill of Lading (BL)
- Commercial Invoice (CI)
- Packing List (PL)
- Marine Insurance Certificate (COI)

Letter of Credit Application (L/C)

Date:

To:

Applicant:
Applicant Reference#:
Beneficiary:
Beneficiary's Advising Bank:

Type of Credit:
Draft:
Expiry Date:

Price Term:
Commodity Description:
Quantity:
Unit Price:
Amount:

Loading Port:
Unlading Port:
Latest Shipping Date:
Partial Shipments:
Transshipment:

Documents:

-
-
-
-

Note:

-
-
-
-

(Sample)

ABC Co., Inc.
1234 A St.
Anytown, USA

Letter of Credit Application (L/C)

Date: 1/1/20XX

To: LA Bank of XYZ, Inc.

Applicant: ABC Co., Inc. 1234 A St., Anytown, USA
Applicant Reference#: PO#1234
Beneficiary: Best Sports, Ltd. 888 Omote-Dori, Yokohama, JAPAN
Beneficiary's Advising Bank: Toto Industrial Bank, 800 Ura-Dori, Yokohama, JAPAN

Type of Credit: Irrevocable
Draft: At Sight
Expiry Date: February 28th, 20XX

Price Term: CIF Port of Los Angeles
Commodity Description: Table Tennis (Ping Pong) Balls
Quantity: 250 Gross (144 count per gross)
Unit Price: USD $40.00 / Gross
Amount: USD $10,000.00

Loading Port: Any Japanese Port
Unlading Port: Los Angeles, USA
Latest Shipping Date: January 31, 20XX
Partial Shipments: Prohibited
Transshipment: Allowed

Documents:

- Full set of on board Bills of Lading marked "Prepaid" and "Notify Applicant"
- Commercial Invoice in triplicate
- Packing List in triplicate
- Marine Insurance Certificate original endorsed in blank for 110% of the invoice value and insurance must include Institute Cargo Clause (C)

Note:

- All banking charges outside the U.S. and remittance charges are for the account of the beneficiary.
- Documents must be presented within 21 days after shipment, but within expiry date.
- This letter of credit is subject to the latest version of the Uniform Customs and Practice for Documentary Credits International Chamber of Commerce (ICC).
- Multi-modal Bill of Lading acceptable.

16

Air Waybill (AWB)
Arrival Notice (A/N)
Bill of Lading (BL)
Booking Request
Cargo Insurance Certificate (COI)
Certificate of Origin (COO)
Commercial Invoice (CI)
Declaration for Free Entry of Returned U.S. Goods (USGR)
Declaration of No Wood Packing Material (WPM)
Declaration of Non-Coniferous Wood Packing Material (WPM)
Entry Summary (Customs Form 7501)
Importer Security Filing Form (ISF)
Importer's Blanket Statement of Non-Reimbursement of
Anti-Dumping Duties (AD/CVD)
Letter of Credit Application (L/C)

Packing List (PL)

Power of Attorney (POA)
Pre-Shipment Inspection Certificate (PSIC)
Pro Forma Invoice
Purchase Order (PO)
Sales Order (SO)
Shipping Instructions (SI)
Telex Release Request (TLX)
Toxic Substances Control Act Statement (TSCA)

Packing List (PL)

ALSO KNOWN AS:
Packing Slip. Weight List.

REQUIRED FOR:
All Imports and Exports

NOT REQUIRED FOR:
N/A

ORIGINAL COPIES NORMALLY REQUIRED?:
No

IN SUMMARY:
The packing list is a shipping document prepared by the shipper that describes the shipment's packaging and may include quantities, weights, dimensions, marks, numbering, and types of packaging.

USEFUL TIPS:
Most customers require an "itemized packing list", which is a packing list that advises the weights of all packaged units. For example, if an ocean container contains 12 pallets of a commodity, then the itemized packing list will show the gross weight (the weight of the entire pallet), the tare weight (the weight of just the pallet and packaging material), and the net weight (the weight of the commodity by itself). And, these three weights would be included on the packing list for all 12 pallets.

WHAT TO REMEMBER:
Information provided on the packing list can and usually will duplicate the information already provided on the commercial invoice for the same shipment. In general, however, the packing list does not normally show the pricing or value of the shipment, but instead provides more detail in regards to how the shipment is packaged.

Packing List

Date:
Invoice#:

Sold To:
Ship To:

Terms of Sale:
Country of Origin and Export:
Actual Mfr:
Freight Charges:

Qty.	Unit	No. Pkg.	Pkg. Dims.	Grs. Wt.	Tare Wt.	Net Wt.	Description of Goods
							Packaging Totals

Marks:

I certify this document to be true and correct.

By: ______________________________ Title: ____________________

(signature)

(Sample)

ABC Co., Inc.
1234 A St.
Anytown, USA

Packing List

Date: 1/1/20XX
Invoice#: 1234

Sold To: Best Sports, Ltd. 888 Omote-Dori, Yokohama, JAPAN
Ship To: (same as above)

Terms of Sale: C&F Yokohama
Country of Origin and Export: USA
Actual Mfr: ABC Co., Inc.
Freight Charges: $1,000.00 USD

Qty.	Unit	No. Pkg.	Pkg. Dims.	Grs. Wt.	Tare Wt.	Net Wt.	Description of Goods
500	Each	500 Boxes	7"x7"x7" (per box)	0.5 Lbs	0.1 Lbs	0.4 Lbs	Basketballs (rubber)
500	Each	500 Boxes	5"x5"x5" (per box)	0.4 Lbs	0.1 Lbs	0.3 Lbs	Volleyballs (synth. leather)
		1000 Boxes		**450 Lbs**	**100 Lbs**	**350 Lbs**	**Packaging Totals**

Marks: "ABC Co., Inc., U.S.A."

I certify this document to be true and correct.

By: ______________________________ Title: ____________________
(signature)

17

Air Waybill (AWB)
Arrival Notice (A/N)
Bill of Lading (BL)
Booking Request
Cargo Insurance Certificate (COI)
Certificate of Origin (COO)
Commercial Invoice (CI)
Declaration for Free Entry of Returned U.S. Goods (USGR)
Declaration of No Wood Packing Material (WPM)
Declaration of Non-Coniferous Wood Packing Material (WPM)
Entry Summary (Customs Form 7501)
Importer Security Filing Form (ISF)
Importer's Blanket Statement of Non-Reimbursement of
Anti-Dumping Duties (AD/CVD)
Letter of Credit Application (L/C)
Packing List (PL)

Power of Attorney (POA)

Pre-Shipment Inspection Certificate (PSIC)
Pro Forma Invoice
Purchase Order (PO)
Sales Order (SO)
Shipping Instructions (SI)
Telex Release Request (TLX)
Toxic Substances Control Act Statement (TSCA)

Power of Attorney (POA)

ALSO KNOWN AS:
POA. Customs Power of Attorney. Import Power of Attorney.

REQUIRED FOR:
All Imports for which the customs clearance services of a customs broker are used.

NOT REQUIRED FOR:
Exports

ORIGINAL COPIES NORMALLY REQUIRED?:
Yes

IN SUMMARY:
The customs power of attorney is a legal document by which the importer (the principal) authorizes a customs broker (the agent/attorney) to perform customs-related business on behalf of the importer.

USEFUL TIPS:
The legal language included in the customs power of attorney will vary somewhat from one customs brokerage operation to the next. The importer may grant a power of attorney to one or several different customs brokerage companies, and it is up to the importer's own discretion to limit (or expand on) a power of attorney to imports at a specific US port, on a specific shipment, within a specified time frame, etc. It should not be necessary to have the POA witnessed or notarized.

WHAT TO REMEMBER:
The customs power of attorney is only to be signed by an individual authorized to sign for the company. The original signed copy of the POA must be mailed to the customs broker for their record keeping requirements. In the case of a partnership, the customs power of attorney will only be effective two years.

Customs Power of Attorney

KNOW ALL PERSONS BY THESE PRESENTS, THAT

____
(Full name of company or individual)

____
(Legal designation, such as corp., individual, sole prop., LLC, or partnership)

Located at

____
(Business Address)

Using EIN or SSN ________________ hereby appoints the agent, ____________________________ as a true and lawful agent and attorney of the principal named above with full power and authority to do and perform every lawful act the said agent and attorney may deem necessary to be done for and on behalf of the said principal without limitation of any kind as fully as said principal could do if present and acting, and hereby ratify and confirm all that said agent and attorney shall lawfully do or cause to be done by virtue of these presents until written notice of revocation is delivered to the agent. In the case of a partnership, this power of attorney will only be effective two years from the date below.

By: ____________________________ Title: ____________________ Date______________
(Principal's signature)

(Sample)

Perfect Customs Brokerage, Inc.
1234 B St.
Anytown, USA

Customs Power of Attorney

KNOW ALL PERSONS BY THESE PRESENTS, THAT

ABC Co., Inc. ____________________________________
(Full name of company or individual)

Corporation ____________________________________
(Legal designation, such as corp., individual, sole prop., LLC, or partnership)

Located at

1234 A St., Anytown, USA____________________________
(Business Address)

Using EIN or SSN XX-XXXXXXX___ hereby appoints the agent,
Perfect Customs Brokerage, Inc., as a true and lawful agent and attorney of the principal named above with full power and authority to do and perform every lawful act the said agent and attorney may deem necessary to be done for and on behalf of the said principal without limitation of any kind as fully as said principal could do if present and acting, and hereby ratify and confirm all that said agent and attorney shall lawfully do or cause to be done by virtue of these presents until written notice of revocation is delivered to the agent. In the case of a partnership, this power of attorney will only be effective two years from the date below.

By: ______________________________ Title: ____________________ Date_____________
(Principal's signature)

18

Air Waybill (AWB)
Arrival Notice (A/N)
Bill of Lading (BL)
Booking Request
Cargo Insurance Certificate (COI)
Certificate of Origin (COO)
Commercial Invoice (CI)
Declaration for Free Entry of Returned U.S. Goods (USGR)
Declaration of No Wood Packing Material (WPM)
Declaration of Non-Coniferous Wood Packing Material (WPM)
Entry Summary (Customs Form 7501)
Importer Security Filing Form (ISF)
Importer's Blanket Statement of Non-Reimbursement of
Anti-Dumping Duties (AD/CVD)
Letter of Credit Application (L/C)
Packing List (PL)
Power of Attorney (POA)

Pre-Shipment Inspection Certificate (PSIC)

Pro Forma Invoice
Purchase Order (PO)
Sales Order (SO)
Shipping Instructions (SI)
Telex Release Request (TLX)
Toxic Substances Control Act Statement (TSCA)

Pre-Shipment Inspection Certificate (PSIC)

ALSO KNOWN AS:
PSIC. Final Random Inspection Certificate.

REQUIRED FOR:
Exports to certain (usually developing) countries

NOT REQUIRED FOR:
N/A

ORIGINAL COPIES NORMALLY REQUIRED?:
Yes

IN SUMMARY:
Pre-Shipment Inspections (PSI) are required by certain importing countries' governments and by some foreign importers in a attempt to best confirm 1) the type of commodity being loaded and shipped, 2) the grade or quality of that commodity, and 3) the resulting accurate valuation of the arranged shipment.

USEFUL TIPS:
Exporters can find details on which countries require pre-shipment inspections as well as a list of private companies normally qualified to conduct pre-shipment inspections at export.gov, a resource for the US trade community and managed by the U.S. Department of Commerce's International Trade Administration.

http://export.gov/logistics/eg_main_018120.asp

WHAT TO REMEMBER:

Exporters should verify with their customer at the time of the order if a pre-shipment inspection certificate (PSIC) is required or not. If an order is inadvertently exported from the seller's country without the necessary pre-shipment inspection, then the shipment will likely be denied by the customer and/or government of the country of importation. Some PSIC inspectors may simply confirm the existence and quality of the material or commodity at the supplier's or consolidator's address. Other inspectors may actually witness the loading process of the goods into the subsequently sealed shipping container or conveyance.

Pre-Shipment Inspection Certificate (PSIC)

Date:
Certificate No.:
Purchase Order No.:

Importer:

Country of Origin and Export:
Container No.:
Seal No.:
Packaging Unit:
Average Weight per Packaging Unit:
Further Details of Import:

Qty.	Unit of Measure	Unit Price	Description of Goods	Total Value (USD)
			Total	

Details of Tests Carried Out:

Declaration:

By: ______________________________ Title: ____________________
(signature)

(Sample)

IAG
It's All Good Inspection Services, Inc.
1212 Check St.
Anytown, USA

Pre-Shipment Inspection Certificate (PSIC)

Date: 1/1/20XX
Certificate No.: IAG1212
Purchase Order No.: 8675309

Importer: Global Sporting Goods, Inc., 123 Sudirman-Thamrin Ave., Jakarta, Indonesia

Country of Origin and Export: USA
Container No.: JSCU9101112
Seal No.: S1234
Packaging Unit: Individual Shoe Boxes
Average Weight per Packaging Unit: 2.0 lbs. net, 0.5 lbs. tare, 2.5 lbs. gross
Further Details of Import:

Qty.	Unit of Measure	Unit Price	Description of Goods	Total Value (USD)
500	Pairs	20.00	Basketball Shoes (size 8)	$10,000.00
500	Pairs	20.00	Basketball Shoes (size 9)	$10,000.00
			Total	**$20,000.00**

Details of Tests Carried Out: Random sampling and visual inspection at time of loading

Declaration:
The consignment as described herein was duly inspected by IAG, Inc. or its authorized agent at ABC Co., Inc. 1234 A St., Anytown, USA on January 1st 20XX. A thorough and random sampling of at least 5% by quantity of the consignment was performed with reasonable care confirming that the contents, quality, and quantity of the consignment are in conformance with the terms of the purchase order 8675309. I hereby certify that the statements made on this document to be true and correct.

By: ______________________________ Title: ____________________
(signature)

19

Air Waybill (AWB)
Arrival Notice (A/N)
Bill of Lading (BL)
Booking Request
Cargo Insurance Certificate (COI)
Certificate of Origin (COO)
Commercial Invoice (CI)
Declaration for Free Entry of Returned U.S. Goods (USGR)
Declaration of No Wood Packing Material (WPM)
Declaration of Non-Coniferous Wood Packing Material (WPM)
Entry Summary (Customs Form 7501)
Importer Security Filing Form (ISF)
Importer's Blanket Statement of Non-Reimbursement of
Anti-Dumping Duties (AD/CVD)
Letter of Credit Application (L/C)
Packing List (PL)
Power of Attorney (POA)
Pre-Shipment Inspection Certificate (PSIC)

Pro Forma Invoice

Purchase Order (PO)
Sales Order (SO)
Shipping Instructions (SI)
Telex Release Request (TLX)
Toxic Substances Control Act Statement (TSCA)

Pro Forma Invoice

ALSO KNOWN AS:
Proforma. Estimate. Dummy Invoice.

REQUIRED FOR:
Imports and Exports requiring a commercial invoice, but one is not yet available for whatever reason.

NOT REQUIRED FOR:
N/A

ORIGINAL COPIES NORMALLY REQUIRED?:
No

IN SUMMARY:
A pro forma invoice may serve two purposes. First, and most common, is temporarily in lieu of an actual commercial invoice for customs purposes (see the section of this handbook titled "Commercial Invoice (CI)". Second, it may be automatically issued by a supplier at the time of the order with the customer, and serve as a sort of sales order (see section titled "Sales Order (SO)".

USEFUL TIPS:
The pro forma invoice should include all of the essential elements of the anticipated commercial invoice such as pricing, quantity, and terms of sale (INCO Terms) in order for customs to accurately assess the actual value of the shipment.

WHAT TO REMEMBER:
Although the pro forma invoice may suffice for US Customs purposes at the time of customs entry, an official commercial invoice must also be obtained from the supplier and maintained on file for recordkeeping requirements.

Pro Forma Invoice

Date:
SO#:

Sold To:
Ship To:

Payment Terms:
Ship by Date:
Ship via:
Terms of Sale:
Country of Origin and Export:
Type of Packaging:

Qty.	Unit of Measure	Unit Price	Description of Goods	Total Value (USD)
			Total	

(Sample)

ABC Co., Inc.
1234 A St.
Anytown, USA

Pro Forma Invoice

Date: 1/1/20XX
SO#: 4321

Sold To: Best Sports, Ltd. 888 Omote-Dori, Yokohama, JAPAN
Ship To: (same as above)

Payment Terms: Documents Against Payment
Ship by Date: 1/31/20XX
Ship via: Ocean Freight
Terms of Sale: C&F Yokohama
Country of Origin and Export: USA
Type of Packaging: Individually boxed for retail sale

Qty.	Unit of Measure	Unit Price	Description of Goods	Total Value (USD)
500	Each	10.00	Basketballs (rubber)	$5,000.00
500	Each	10.00	Volleyballs (synth. leather)	$5,000.00
			Total	**$10,000.00**

20

Air Waybill (AWB)
Arrival Notice (A/N)
Bill of Lading (BL)
Booking Request
Cargo Insurance Certificate (COI)
Certificate of Origin (COO)
Commercial Invoice (CI)
Declaration for Free Entry of Returned U.S. Goods (USGR)
Declaration of No Wood Packing Material (WPM)
Declaration of Non-Coniferous Wood Packing Material (WPM)
Entry Summary (Customs Form 7501)
Importer Security Filing Form (ISF)
Importer's Blanket Statement of Non-Reimbursement of
    Anti-Dumping Duties (AD/CVD)
Letter of Credit Application (L/C)
Packing List (PL)
Power of Attorney (POA)
Pre-Shipment Inspection Certificate (PSIC)
Pro Forma Invoice

Purchase Order (PO)

Sales Order (SO)
Shipping Instructions (SI)
Telex Release Request (TLX)
Toxic Substances Control Act Statement (TSCA)

Purchase Order (PO)

ALSO KNOWN AS:
PO. Purchase Agreement. International Purchase Agreement. Purchase Contract. PC.

REQUIRED FOR:
The origin of all Imports and Exports

NOT REQUIRED FOR:
N/A

ORIGINAL COPIES NORMALLY REQUIRED?:
No

IN SUMMARY:
The flip side of a sales order, a purchase order is a document issued by the buyer/customer to the seller/supplier outlining the specifics of a proposed transfer of a good and/or service.

USEFUL TIPS:
For the purpose of clarity and to avoid any potential misunderstandings, the purchase order can include as much detail as possible, including, but of course not limited to the international commercial terms (Incoterms), quantity and detailed description of the product, packaging, purchase price, payment terms, and any additional general terms and conditions of the transaction deemed necessary.

WHAT TO REMEMBER:
Although also known as a purchase contract, the purchase order is not a legally binding contract until it is signed by or otherwise accepted by the selling party. Also, even though most international transactions are confirmed in US dollars (USD), it is essential that both parties are in agreement on the remittance currency to be used.

Purchase Order

Date:
PO#:

Vendor Name:

Sold To:
Ship To:

Payment Terms:
Ship by Date:
Ship via:
Terms of Sale:
Country of Origin and Export:
Type of Packaging:

Qty.	Unit of Measure	Unit Price	Description of Goods	Total Value (USD)
			Total	

The undersigned seller hereby acknowledges and agrees to the foregoing offer in accordance with the terms and conditions specified above.

By: ______________________________ Date: ____________________

(signature of seller)

(Sample)

Best Sports, Ltd.
888 Omote-Dori,
Yokohama, JAPAN

Purchase Order

Date: 1/1/20XX
PO#: 1234

Vendor Name: ABC Co., Inc.

Sold To: Best Sports, Ltd. 888 Omote-Dori, Yokohama, JAPAN
Ship To: (same as above)

Payment Terms: Documents Against Payment
Ship by Date: 1/31/20XX
Ship via: Air Freight
Terms of Sale: C&F Yokohama
Country of Origin and Export: USA
Type of Packaging: Individually boxed for retail sale

Qty.	Unit of Measure	Unit Price	Description of Goods	Total Value (USD)
500	Each	10.00	Basketballs (rubber)	$5,000.00
500	Each	10.00	Volleyballs (synth. leather)	$5,000.00
			Total	**$10,000.00**

The undersigned seller hereby acknowledges and agrees to the foregoing offer in accordance with the terms and conditions specified above.

By: ______________________________ Date: ____________________
(signature of seller)

21

Air Waybill (AWB)
Arrival Notice (A/N)
Bill of Lading (BL)
Booking Request
Cargo Insurance Certificate (COI)
Certificate of Origin (COO)
Commercial Invoice (CI)
Declaration for Free Entry of Returned U.S. Goods (USGR)
Declaration of No Wood Packing Material (WPM)
Declaration of Non-Coniferous Wood Packing Material (WPM)
Entry Summary (Customs Form 7501)
Importer Security Filing Form (ISF)
Importer's Blanket Statement of Non-Reimbursement of
Anti-Dumping Duties (AD/CVD)
Letter of Credit Application (L/C)
Packing List (PL)
Power of Attorney (POA)
Pre-Shipment Inspection Certificate (PSIC)
Pro Forma Invoice
Purchase Order (PO)

Sales Order (SO)

Shipping Instructions (SI)
Telex Release Request (TLX)
Toxic Substances Control Act Statement (TSCA)

Sales Order (SO)

ALSO KNOWN AS:
SO. Sales Agreement. International Sales Agreement. Sales Contract. SC.

REQUIRED FOR:
The origin of all Imports and Exports

NOT REQUIRED FOR:
N/A

ORIGINAL COPIES NORMALLY REQUIRED?:
No

IN SUMMARY:
The flip side of a purchase order, a sales order is a document issued by the seller/supplier to the buyer/customer outlining the specifics of a proposed transfer of a good and/or service.

USEFUL TIPS:
For the purpose of clarity and to avoid any potential misunderstandings, the sales order can include as much detail as possible, including, but of course not limited to the international commercial terms (Incoterms), quantity and detailed description of the product, packaging, purchase price, payment terms, and any additional general terms and conditions of the transaction deemed necessary.

WHAT TO REMEMBER:
Although also known as a sales contract, the sales order is not a legally binding contract until it is signed by or otherwise accepted by the purchasing party. Also, even though most international transactions are confirmed in US dollars (USD), it is essential that both parties are in agreement on the remittance currency to be used.

Sales Order

Date:
SO#:

Sold To:
Ship To:

Payment Terms:
Ship by Date:
Ship via:
Terms of Sale:
Country of Origin and Export:
Type of Packaging:

Qty.	Unit of Measure	Unit Price	Description of Goods	Total Value (USD)
			Total	

The undersigned buyer hereby acknowledges and agrees to the foregoing offer in accordance with the terms and conditions specified above.

By: ______________________________ Date: ____________________
(signature of buyer)

(Sample)

ABC Co., Inc.
1234 A St.
Anytown, USA

Sales Order

Date: 1/1/20XX
SO#: 4321

Sold To: Best Sports, Ltd. 888 Omote-Dori, Yokohama, JAPAN
Ship To: (same as above)

Payment Terms: Documents Against Payment
Ship by Date: 1/31/20XX
Ship via: Ocean Freight
Terms of Sale: C&F Yokohama
Country of Origin and Export: USA
Type of Packaging: Individually boxed for retail sale

Qty.	Unit of Measure	Unit Price	Description of Goods	Total Value (USD)
500	Each	10.00	Basketballs (rubber)	$5,000.00
500	Each	10.00	Volleyballs (synth. leather)	$5,000.00
			Total	**$10,000.00**

The undersigned buyer hereby acknowledges and agrees to the foregoing offer in accordance with the terms and conditions specified above.

By: ______________________________ Date: ____________________

(signature of buyer)

22

Air Waybill (AWB)
Arrival Notice (A/N)
Bill of Lading (BL)
Booking Request
Cargo Insurance Certificate (COI)
Certificate of Origin (COO)
Commercial Invoice (CI)
Declaration for Free Entry of Returned U.S. Goods (USGR)
Declaration of No Wood Packing Material (WPM)
Declaration of Non-Coniferous Wood Packing Material (WPM)
Entry Summary (Customs Form 7501)
Importer Security Filing Form (ISF)
Importer's Blanket Statement of Non-Reimbursement of
Anti-Dumping Duties (AD/CVD)
Letter of Credit Application (L/C)
Packing List (PL)
Power of Attorney (POA)
Pre-Shipment Inspection Certificate (PSIC)
Pro Forma Invoice
Purchase Order (PO)
Sales Order (SO)

Shipping Instructions (SI)

Telex Release Request (TLX)
Toxic Substances Control Act Statement (TSCA)

Shipping Instructions (SI)

ALSO KNOWN AS:
S.I. BL Instructions. International Shipping Instructions. Shipper's Letter of Instructions. S.L.I.

REQUIRED FOR:
All Exports

NOT REQUIRED FOR:
Imports

ORIGINAL COPIES NORMALLY REQUIRED?:
No

IN SUMMARY:
Shipping instructions are detailed instructions that a shipper provides to their carrier in order for the carrier to accurately draft and issue an export's bill of lading. Information provided by the exporter includes shipper contact details, consignee details, the bill to party and whether freight charges will be prepaid or collect, description of goods, weights, packaging, etc.

USEFUL TIPS:
If a carrier requires shipping instructions before the exact details are known, the shipper may have to estimate some information such as weights, etc. for them (also known as "dummy instructions") and then provide the carrier the missing details as soon as possible afterwards.

WHAT TO REMEMBER:
At the time of booking your export with your carrier, verify the actual deadline (date and time) for the submittal of shipping instructions. If the S.I. is late, your shipment may not make the vessel or flight as scheduled. Also, confirm with your freight forwarder if they can submit an export declaration (also known as AES) on your behalf. If they cannot, or if you are not using the services of a freight forwarder, then an Internal Transaction Number (ITN) will also be a required element of your S.I. Go to www.aesdirect.gov and www.bis.doc.gov to learn more regarding certain export requirements.

Shipping Instructions

Date:

Booking#:
ITN#:

Shipper:
Shipper's Export Reference:
Consignee:
Notify Party:
Country of Origin:

Port of Loading:
Port of Discharge:
Final Destination:

Description of Goods:
Marks:
Container No.:
No. and Type of Packages:

Pallet	No. of Pkgs.	Pallet. Dims.	Grs. Wt.	Tare Wt.	Net Wt.
Totals					

Value of Shipment (USD):
Ocean Freight:
Destination Charges:
Cargo Insurance Required?:
Original Bills of Lading Required?:

(Sample)

ABC Co., Inc.
1234 A St.
Anytown, USA

Shipping Instructions

Date: 1/1/20XX

Booking#: JSCU12345678
ITN#: N/A

Shipper: ABC Co., Inc. 1234 A St., Anytown, USA
Shipper's Export Reference: PO#1234
Consignee: Best Sports, Ltd. 888 Omote-Dori, Yokohama, JAPAN
Notify Party: Same as Consignee
Country of Origin: USA

Port of Loading: Los Angeles
Port of Discharge: Yokohama
Final Destination: Yokohama

Description of Goods: Sports Equipment (Basketballs & Volleyballs)
Marks: "ABC Co., Inc., USA"
Container No.: JSCU1234567
No. and Type of Packages: 1000 Boxes on 2 Pallets (see below)

Pallet	No. of Pkgs.	Pallet. Dims.	Grs. Wt.	Tare Wt.	Net Wt.
#1	500 Boxes	40"x40"x40"	250 Lbs	60 Lbs	190 Lbs
#2	500 Boxes	40"x40"x30"	200 Lbs	40 Lbs	160 Lbs
Totals	**1000 Boxes**	**On 2 Pallets**	**450 Lbs**	**100 Lbs**	**350 Lbs**

Value of Shipment (USD): $10,000.00
Ocean Freight: Prepaid
Destination Charges: Collect
Cargo Insurance Required?: No.
Original Bills of Lading Required?: Yes.

23

Air Waybill (AWB)
Arrival Notice (A/N)
Bill of Lading (BL)
Booking Request
Cargo Insurance Certificate (COI)
Certificate of Origin (COO)
Commercial Invoice (CI)
Declaration for Free Entry of Returned U.S. Goods (USGR)
Declaration of No Wood Packing Material (WPM)
Declaration of Non-Coniferous Wood Packing Material (WPM)
Entry Summary (Customs Form 7501)
Importer Security Filing Form (ISF)
Importer's Blanket Statement of Non-Reimbursement of
Anti-Dumping Duties (AD/CVD)
Letter of Credit Application (L/C)
Packing List (PL)
Power of Attorney (POA)
Pre-Shipment Inspection Certificate (PSIC)
Pro Forma Invoice
Purchase Order (PO)
Sales Order (SO)
Shipping Instructions (SI)

Telex Release Request (TLX)

Toxic Substances Control Act Statement (TSCA)

Telex Release Request (TLX)

ALSO KNOWN OR REFERRED TO AS:
BL Surrender Request. Waybill Release Request. Express Release Request.

REQUIRED FOR:
Exports for which exporter/shipper has confirmed receipt of payment from the customer and is ready to surrender control and ownership of the cargo to their customer.

NOT REQUIRED FOR:
N/A

ORIGINAL COPIES NORMALLY REQUIRED?:
No

IN SUMMARY:
The telex release request is an official request by the shipper and addressed to the shipping company. It authorizes the shipping company to release the shipment to the consignee at destination as notated on the Bill of Lading.

USEFUL TIPS:
The telex release request is not actually sent via a telex machine (an antiquated form of international telegraphic correspondence). Acceptable formats of the telex release request from the shipper will differ somewhat from carrier to carrier. Some carriers may accept the telex release request via a brief email, while others may require the request to be typed up on a carrier-supplied letter template and then sent as an email attachment.

WHAT TO REMEMBER:
Some customers may request their supplier (the shipper) to telex release the cargo to them prior to the shipper actually receiving payment. This practice is very risky since the supplier no longer maintains control of the shipment once it has been released to the consignee. However, once payment has officially been received by the shipper from the overseas customer, the telex release is a quicker method of releasing the goods to the customer than physically couriering original bills of lading to their foreign office.

Telex Release Request (TLX)

To:

We, ______________________ confirm and hereby authorize the telex release of the below mentioned shipment for which we surrender full sets of original bills of lading. You are kindly requested to release this cargo accordingly to the below mentioned "release to" party. Please duly notify the appropriate parties at destination regarding this cargo release. Thank you for your cooperation.

Shipment# (BL#, AWB#, or Booking#):
Container#:
"Release To" Party:

Return receipt requested.

By: ______________________________ Title: ____________________ Date_____________
(Shipper's signature)

(Sample)

ABC Co., Inc.
1234 A St.
Anytown, USA

Telex Release Request (TLX)

To: Joe's Shipping Co.

We, ABC Co., Inc. ______ confirm and hereby authorize the telex release of the below mentioned shipment for which we surrender full sets of original bills of lading. You are kindly requested to release this cargo accordingly to the below mentioned "release to" party. Please duly notify the appropriate parties at destination regarding this cargo release. Thank you for your cooperation.

Shipment# (BL#, AWB#, or Booking#): BL# JSCU12345678
Container#: JSCU1234567
"Release To" Party: Best Sports, Ltd. 888 Omote-Dori, Yokohama, JAPAN

Return receipt requested.

By: ______________________________ Title: ____________________ Date_____________
(Shipper's signature)

24

Air Waybill (AWB)
Arrival Notice (A/N)
Bill of Lading (BL)
Booking Request
Cargo Insurance Certificate (COI)
Certificate of Origin (COO)
Commercial Invoice (CI)
Declaration for Free Entry of Returned U.S. Goods (USGR)
Declaration of No Wood Packing Material (WPM)
Declaration of Non-Coniferous Wood Packing Material (WPM)
Entry Summary (Customs Form 7501)
Importer Security Filing Form (ISF)
Importer's Blanket Statement of Non-Reimbursement of
Anti-Dumping Duties (AD/CVD)
Letter of Credit Application (L/C)
Packing List (PL)
Power of Attorney (POA)
Pre-Shipment Inspection Certificate (PSIC)
Pro Forma Invoice
Purchase Order (PO)
Sales Order (SO)
Shipping Instructions (SI)
Telex Release Request (TLX)

Toxic Substances Control Act Statement (TSCA)

Toxic Substances Control Act Statement (TSCA)

ALSO KNOWN AS:
Toxic Substances Control Act of 1976. TSCA.

REQUIRED FOR:
Imports and Exports containing chemicals (see the EPA's website for details www.epa.gov).

NOT REQUIRED FOR:
Exempt items (see the EPA's website for details www.epa.gov).

ORIGINAL COPIES NORMALLY REQUIRED?:
No

IN SUMMARY:
TSCA is a US law that regulates, among other things, the importation and exportation of chemicals and chemical-related merchandise and is administered by the Environmental Protection Agency (EPA). As it relates to importers and exporters, the TSCA Statement or TSCA Certification is a document that the US seller or US buyer must complete by A) certifying that their shipment either complies with TSCA rules or B) by certifying that their shipment is not subject to TSCA.

USEFUL TIPS:
Listed below are examples of items that require a completed TSCA Statement...

- Pigments, dyes, and ink
- Plastics in primary forms
- Soaps
- Lubricants
- Waxes
- Paint
- Cleaners, detergents, and air fresheners

WHAT TO REMEMBER:
If you need assistance regarding the TSCA applicability of your shipment, contact the TSCA Hotline at (202) 554-1404 and/or consult with your customs broker.

Toxic Substances Control Act Statement (TSCA)

Check the box corresponding to the applicable statement below (check only one):

Positive Statement:

☐ I certify that all chemical substances in this shipment comply with all applicable rules or orders under TSCA and that I am not offering a chemical substance for entry in violation of TSCA or any applicable rule or order there under.

Negative Statement:

☐ I certify that all chemical substances in this shipment are not subject to TSCA.

Authorized Name (please print): ______________________________

Authorized Signature: ______________________________

Title: ____________________________

Shipment Ref#: ____________________________

(Sample)

ABC Co., Inc.
1234 A St.
Anytown, USA

Toxic Substances Control Act Statement (TSCA)

Check the box corresponding to the applicable statement below (check only one):

Positive Statement:

☐ I certify that all chemical substances in this shipment comply with all applicable rules or orders under TSCA and that I am not offering a chemical substance for entry in violation of TSCA or any applicable rule or order there under.

Negative Statement:

☑ I certify that all chemical substances in this shipment are not subject to TSCA.

Authorized Name (please print): ______________________________

Authorized Signature: ______________________________

Title: ____________________________

Shipment Ref#: ____________________________

25
References

AES Direct Home Page.
http://www.aesdirect.gov/
Accessed 2013.

American Institute of Marine Underwriters Home Page.
http://www.aimu.org/
Accessed 2013.

Export.gov Home Page.
http://export.gov/
Accessed 2013.

Hinkelman, Edward G., *Dictionary of International Trade*, World Trade Press, California, 1994.

International Air Transport Association Home Page.
https://www.iata.org/
Accessed 2013.

International Chamber of Commerce Home Page.
http://www.iccwbo.org/
Accessed 2013.

Manresa, Maritza, *How to Open & Operate a Financially Successful Import Export Business*, Atlantic Publishing Group, Inc., Florida, 2010.

Turner, Krista, *Start Your Own Import/Export Business*, Entrepreneur Media Inc., 2010.

U.S. Customs and Border Protection Home Page.
http://www.cbp.gov/
Accessed 2013.

U.S. Government Printing Office Home Page.
Title 19 Electronic Code of Federal Regulations "Customs Duties"
http://www.ecfr.gov/
Accessed 2013.

United States Department of Agriculture Home Page.
Animal and Plant Health Inspection Service
http://www.aphis.usda.gov/
Accessed 2013.

United States Environment Protection Agency Home Page.
http://www.epa.gov/
Accessed 2013.

United States International Trade Commission Home Page
"Harmonized Tariff Schedule of the United States"
January 1, 2013 edition
http://www.usitc.gov/
Accessed 2013.

26
Index

D

E

F

H

I

L

M

N

O

P

R

Made in United States
Orlando, FL
04 November 2026

90200289R00059